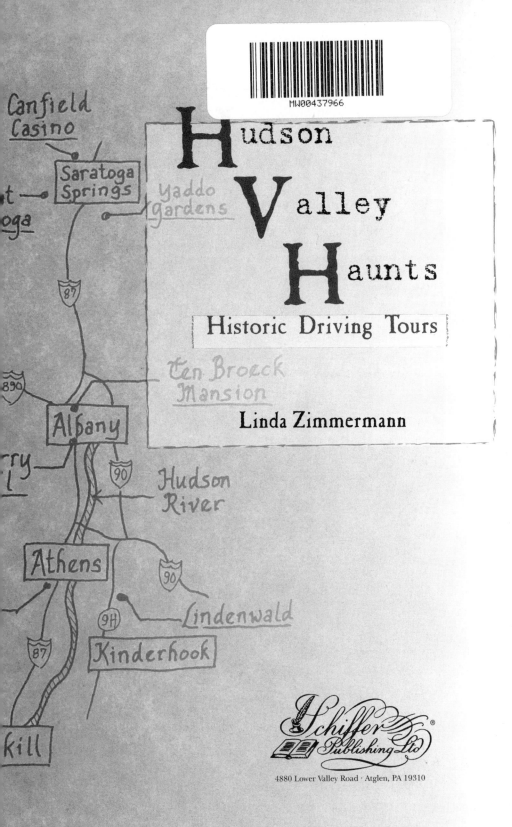

Canfield
Casino

Saratoga
Springs

Yaddo
gardens

t —
oga

87

890

Albany

rry
l

90

Hudson
River

Athens

90

9H

Lindenwald

87

Kinderhook

kill

Hudson Valley Haunts

Historic Driving Tours

Ten Broeck
Mansion

Linda Zimmermann

Schiffer Publishing Ltd.

4880 Lower Valley Road · Atglen, PA 19310

Schiffer Books are available at special discounts for bulk purchases for sales promotions or premiums. Special editions, including personalized covers, corporate imprints, and excerpts can be created in large quantities for special needs. For more information contact the publisher:

Published by Schiffer Publishing Ltd.
4880 Lower Valley Road
Atglen, PA 19310
Phone: (610) 593-1777; Fax: (610) 593-2002
E-mail: Info@schifferbooks.com

For the largest selection of fine reference books on this and related subjects, please visit our web site at **www.schifferbooks.com**
We are always looking for people to write books on new and related subjects. If you have an idea for a book please contact us at the above address.

This book may be purchased from the publisher.
Include $5.00 for shipping.
Please try your bookstore first.
You may write for a free catalog.

In Europe, Schiffer books are distributed by
Bushwood Books
6 Marksbury Ave.
Kew Gardens
Surrey TW9 4JF England
Phone: 44 (0) 20 8392-8585; Fax: 44 (0) 20 8392-9876
E-mail: info@bushwoodbooks.co.uk
Website: www.bushwoodbooks.co.uk
Free postage in the U.K., Europe; air mail at cost.

Copyright © 2009 by Linda Zimmermann
Library of Congress Control Number: 2008943092

Designed by RoS
Type set in Batik Regular/New Baskerville BT

ISBN: 978-0-7643-3173-2

Printed in The United States of America

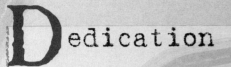

Dedication

To all who

dedicate themselves

to preserving

the true *spirit*

of the Hudson Valley.

Contents

Author's Note

The idea for this project had been brewing for some time. As a lifelong Hudson Valley resident, I have always been fascinated by the history of the region. For many years I have written and lectured about the four centuries of the valley's people, places, and events, so this book is a natural evolution of my previous work.

In another aspect, and one that is often viewed as being supernatural, I have also been captivated by ghost stories from the time I first read the books of Hans Holzer by flashlight under the covers when I was supposed to be sleeping. For more than a decade now, I have been personally investigating and writing about haunted sites, primarily in the Hudson Valley.

To combine these interests for this book has been a great pleasure, full of fun and marvelous experiences. Unfortunately, not every site wished to participate in this ghostly tour, unsure of how the public would take to the more shadowy side of their history. So don't be alarmed if you don't see every site (or every ghost) you may expect to see—at least this time. I'm still working on it, and hope they all come on board in the future.

I still encourage you to visit the sites not listed here, and perhaps remind them that our nation's most historic home—the White House in Washington, D.C.—openly speaks about the ghost in the Lincoln bedroom. (And I think such stories enhance, rather than sully, the history, don't you?)

By far, the outpouring of support for this book was wonderful. My heartfelt thanks go out to the site managers and staff, historical societies, libraries, and all the dedicated volunteers who help preserve and share our history. Hopefully, it has been a mutually beneficial endeavor, as some locations discovered new aspects of their sites and gained a deeper appreciation of the people involved with its past.

I must also express my gratitude to Barbara Bleitzhofer, who helped get this project up and running by contacting scores of places up and down the Hudson, and kept the ensuing mass of information expertly organized. You're the best, Barb!

It seems that no book project of mine is complete without a road trip with Michael Worden. This time we skillfully managed to find almost the same number of places to eat as we did visits to historic sites. And yes, there was a sufficient supply of brownies for the trip.

Thanks also to Dr. Art Donohue who took time from his vacation to act as investigative reporter and obtain some key photographs.

I must also make special mention of Bruce Janicki, who helped out on a photo shoot right after I had a particularly rough session at the dentist. (I think the Novocain has finally just about worn off…)

And as always, many thanks to my husband, Bob Strong, who tirelessly offers "whatever help you need." I was particularly happy to be able to include his hand-drawn section maps instead of some dull computer-generated graphics.

Thanks also to my editor, Dinah Roseberry, whose interest in the paranormal and enthusiasm for the book idea convinced me to undertake this project. May there be many more!

Finally a word to the readers: Even though I have lived my entire life in the Hudson Valley, I was surprised at how many amazing places there were to see. Please take the time to visit these sites and take the tours. Each one has fascinating stories about the men and women who lived and died there, and it is these personal details that bring these places to life.

Then, of course, there is the afterlife part of their stories. In this regard, I encourage skeptics to keep an open mind, and believers to not let their imaginations run wild. Let these historic places speak for themselves. They all have many stories to tell, for those willing to listen…

Linda Zimmermann
Hudson Valley, July 2008

Introduction

The valley through which the Hudson River flows may just be one of America's best-kept secrets. Its combination of beauty and history are arguably unsurpassed in this country. Throughout the centuries, the Hudson River has been viewed in many lights, from being a place of danger, to a gateway to profit, to a key to liberty, to a romanticized vision of unspoiled nature, to a place to dump toxic waste. In short, it has truly been many things to many different people.

On paper, the statistics aren't very impressive—only 315 miles long from its highest source in Lake Tear of the Clouds on the southwest slope of Mount Marcy in the Adirondacks, south to its end in New York Harbor, it ranks a mere 71st in length among U.S. rivers. At its widest point at Haverstraw it is 3.5 miles, and near West Point at World's End, it reaches its greatest depth of 216 feet. However, statistics often fail to give an accurate picture and they don't speak to the importance of this modest waterway to the development of our country.

For thousands of years, Native Americans camped along the shores of the river, but the beginning of their end came in 1609 with Henry Hudson. In an attempt to find a passage to China, Hudson received funding from the Dutch East India Company. In his ship, the *Halfmoon*, Hudson traveled upriver as far as Albany before he realized he wasn't going to reach China that way. Even in failure, however, the Dutch realized there was much to be gained in this region and they began to settle on Manhattan Island, and soon cast their eyes and ambitions upriver.

The river was dangerous to navigate, especially between Peekskill and Newburgh, and the dense forests and native populations were viewed with equal trepidation, but slowly the Dutch established other large settlements such as Albany and Kingston, and many other smaller communities. There were frequent Indian wars and all manner of hardships, but they persevered. In 1664, the English seized control of New York, but Dutch customs and styles persisted for generations.

The English way of life progressed for a century, until something new began to stir—the desire to live an American way of life. In the struggle for independence, the Hudson River was viewed as a vital artery of communications and supplies between the northern and southern colonies. The British knew that severing that artery would be the key to eventual victory. As a result, the Hudson Valley became the scene of many dramatic and crucial events—the Battles of Saratoga, and Forts Montgomery and Clinton, Benedict Arnold's treason, the burning of Kingston, and the frequent bloody conflicts between loyalist and patriot neighbors.

The next revolution to hit the valley was one of an industrial nature. When Fulton's steamboat made its first trip up the Hudson River in 1807, it opened the floodgates to commercial opportunities. New York City grew on Haverstraw Bricks and Rosendale cement, was fed by the valley's farms, and kept its food fresh with Rockland Lake ice. With urban development came the desire to escape "to the country," and tourism became an industry unto itself. While the common folk spent summers in hotels and cottages along the river, the wealthy built grand mansions.

Unfortunately, what goes boom often goes bust and the twentieth century began to see a decline in many Hudson Valley communities. With the post-WWII baby boom and demand for affordable housing, many important old homes were leveled by developers with little regard for history. Once thriving downtowns became blighted areas and industrial waste flowed freely into the river, as in the case of General Electric which pumped over a million pounds of PCBs into the Hudson. The impact of decades worth of this neglect and abuse are still with us today.

Fortunately, in recent years there has been yet another twist and turn in the river's history as pollution levels are down, decaying properties are being restored, and preservation of historic sites has gained recognition. Of course, there is still much work to be done, but much can be accomplished by simply raising the awareness of the Hudson Valley treasures still left to us.

This book presents a wide array of sites that represent hundreds of years of the valley's people and events. From stunning mansions to humble dwellings, from ancient Indian sites to Revolutionary War battlefields, these places provide fascinating pictures of the triumphs and struggles of those who lived here before us.

This book also provides a unique perspective other histories often neglect—the tangible aftereffects of those struggles, which often lingers in such places for generations. The footsteps heard late at night, the door that closes on its own, the shadowy figure that lurks in the corner, these are all equally important parts of the stories of these sites.

Some places refuse to even mention the "g-word," but ghosts have always been part of the folklore and beliefs of the people of the valley, from the Indians, to the Dutch, to the English, to the scores of different nationalities that poured into the region. Each culture inherited the stories that came before them, and then added to and enhanced the "spirit" of our local lore. To deny such things exist is to turn a blind eye to centuries of personal encounters.

Of course, not all ghost stories are created equal. There are the old tales passed from generation to generation until no one can be certain of the original facts, if there indeed ever were any. Then there are the remarkable cases where independent witnesses with no prior knowledge of a place have the same experiences. In some instances, figures are seen that can even be later identified as previous owners. Such cases are rare, however, and for the most part, the unusual sights and sounds remain mysterious, yet undeniable, pieces of a puzzle.

Which is not to say these puzzles can't be solved, and perhaps it will be the readers of this book who will help unlock the many mysteries. Was there a tragic death at the site that causes the unhappy spirit to linger? What regrets, what unrequited loves, what discontented lives have led to the ghosts that still walk the halls of such places? Or are some of these more contented spirits, the spirits of those who loved their homes so much in life, they choose to remain in them even after death?

What greater adventure can there be then to visit such a site, explore the rich history of its people and the events, and then see if you can discover any deeper secrets from the other world, where a passing shadow or faint whisper may signal that you have just had an encounter in the haunted Hudson Valley.

Section One

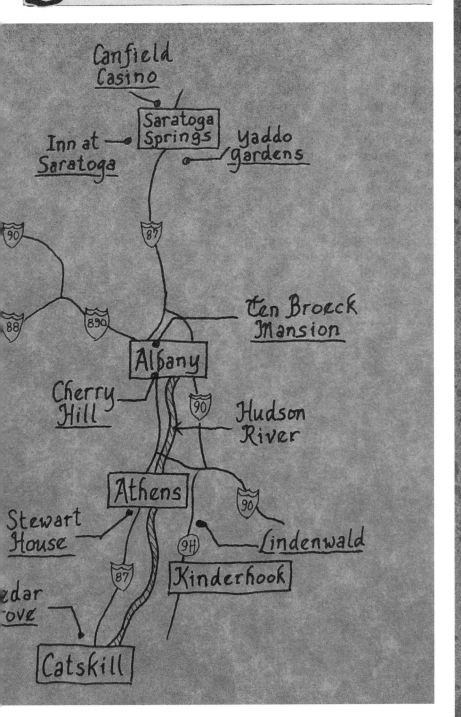

One of the historic jewels of the Hudson Valley is the mansion of Lindenwald in Kinderhook. For over 200 years, many fascinating people passed through its doors. The place has been the scene of high stakes political wheeling and dealing, as well as a being a wager in a high-stakes card game in which the house itself was lost. It was also the home of a president, a suicidal butler, and a tyrannical cook—any or all of who may still walk the halls and grounds.

Kinderhook was an early Dutch settlement and its name means "children's corner." It was a favorite haunt (of the living variety) of author Washington Irving, and it was Kinderhook's teacher upon whom he based the famous character of Ichabod Crane. Irving also drew inspiration from other people and places in Kinderhook, and its local legend of a headless horseman, for the most famous ghost story in American literature, *The Legend of Sleepy Hollow*.

The town is also known as the birthplace of the eighth president of the United States, Martin Van Buren, who was born there in 1782. He was to return to Kinderhook after he left the White House, but there is a little more history to fill in before we attend to the president.

Lindenwald
The Martin Van Buren National Historic Site

The mansion of Lindenwald in Kinderhook, the former home
of President Martin Van Buren.

Lindenwald was named by Van Buren for the linden trees along the old post road in front of the house. The original structure was built by Judge William Peter Van Ness in the year 1797. The structure began life as a more modest brick Dutch farmhouse, but would see extensive remodeling and expansion over the years. The son of the original builder, William "Billy" Van Ness, gained fame, or infamy as the case may be, during a duel in which he acted as the second for former Vice-President Aaron Burr. The duel in question was the tragic episode that resulted in Burr killing Alexander Hamilton. Hamilton's death deprived the young American nation of one of its truly great and dynamic intellectuals. It also turned up the heat under an already unpopular Aaron Burr who sought to drop out of sight until things cooled down.

For many years, it was suspected that after the murder of Hamilton, Burr fled to Lindenwald where he was to hide out for three years. Supposed evidence of this was the discovery of a secret, windowless room, in the early 1900s. While the roof was being replaced, the secret room was revealed and the owner, one Dr. Birney, somewhat ungallantly lowered his own daughter into the dark room, suspended on a rope, to investigate. According to Dr. Birney, the room was empty except for three items, a small toy pig, a little rocking chair, and Aaron Burr's personal calling card. This flimsy "proof" of the presence of Burr's calling card did not hold up to scrutiny. As tempting as it is to imagine Burr hiding for three years in this dark, secret room, it turns out that this room had not even been built during the time of his alleged stay at Lindenwald.

However, even though presently there is no evidence to substantiate these earlier claims, the ghost of Aaron Burr has nonetheless been spotted several times. Eyewitnesses describe Burr, wearing a maroon-colored coat and lace ruffles that *did not* move in the breeze, walking slowly through the orchard. Unfortunately, the orchard no longer exists, but the National Parks system does have plans to restore it. Perhaps when the trees are growing again, Burr will resume his midnight walks?

After having served as president of the United States, Martin Van Buren retired and decided to move back to Kinderhook. He was a friend of the Van Ness family and was familiar with their home at Lindenwald and decided that it was there he wanted to spend his remaining years. Van Buren was able to persuade Billy Van Ness to sell the house and the ex-president soon made it his home. Calling upon Richard Upjohn, the architect for Trinity Church in New York City, Van Buren ordered extensive remodeling and expansion. Inside and out, Lindenwald became a showplace of wealth and refinement. However, despite the time and energy Van Buren poured into the house, it is in the orchard that his ghost was allegedly seen.

This same apple orchard is also the location for yet another of Lindenwald's shadowy apparitions. Van Buren apparently had in his employ a butler who seemed to make liberal use of the contents of the liquor cabinet. Whether from an alcohol-induced depression, or for some other unknown reason, the unhappy butler chose to hang himself from one of the apple trees. While the orchard was still standing, witnesses claimed to see the figure of the deceased butler swinging in one of the trees.

A more recent ghost was also glimpsed on the mansion grounds. In the middle of the twentieth century, there were reports that a woman had been murdered near Lindenwald's gatehouse, and the poor victim's white apparition has been seen in the vicinity ever since.

While few properties can boast such famous spirits as the ghost of a president and the murderer of Alexander Hamilton, the house itself is not to be outdone. Several generations of private owners have heard footsteps and slamming doors when no one else was in the house. As for the doors themselves, they are massive, made of solid wood and are mounted on sturdy hinges. It is unlikely that such doors would open and close on their own. And while creaking floorboards can be expected in such an old house, eyewitnesses insist that the sounds were clearly those of *footsteps*, not creaking wood. One theory as to originator of these footsteps involves the son of Martin Van Buren.

"Prince" John Van Buren was a spoiled, hard drinking gambler. Legend has it that his father had to fill in the fishpond that was on the estate because his drunken son too often fell into it. After his father passed away, Prince John continued his dissolute lifestyle and actually ended up losing the Lindenwald mansion in a card game! (In an interesting twist, he had also bet his mistress along with the house, but history does not record whether she honored his gambling debt.) Some people believe that Prince John still walks the corridors and slams the doors of the home he loved, and so abruptly and foolishly lost.

The lucky card player who won Lindenwald was a man by the name of Leonard Jerome from New York City. Jerome owned several properties in the area, and it is doubtful whether he actually resided at Lindenwald, but it is worth mentioning him because of one of his daughters, Jennie. As was the fashion in those days, Jennie was sent to England, ostensibly to learn culture and refinement, but more likely to snag a wealthy and influential husband.

In the latter regard, her trip was a great success, and one that was to play a major role in the history of the world. Jennie Jerome was able to catch the eye of an English aristocrat and they were married.

This daughter of a former owner of Lindenwald gave birth to a son. This boy was none other than Winston Churchill, a man who steadfastly led his nation out of its darkest hour. Perhaps some of his spunk had been derived from his New York gambler grandfather. In any event, it is just one more interesting piece of history that makes this region so fascinating.

Getting back to the ghosts, we come across the unusual and amusing character of Aunt Sarah. There are unsubstantiated reports that the skeletons of fifteen slaves are buried in the wine cellar, although Van Buren himself did not own slaves. However, there were many free African-Americans in the area, and several were on Lindenwald's staff during his years there, according to a former Director of the NYS Historical Association. The most memorable was Aunt Sarah, the cook, who ruled her basement kitchen as a sovereign territory, not to be trespassed by anyone. Whenever it was necessary for someone else to enter her domain, the visit was always brief and with her consent.

Such dictatorial behavior was no doubt tolerated because Aunt Sarah was a cook of extraordinary abilities. But as all good things must end, after many years of producing fabulous meals, Aunt Sarah passed away. However, it is just possible that not even death could keep the talented but ornery Aunt Sarah from attending to her duties in the kitchen.

For several years in the long history of Lindenwald, the house was vacant. A nearby neighbor, a Mrs. Wagner, took it upon herself to keep an eye on the house and property. When she was informed that new owners were planning to move in, she instructed her servant, Tom, to clean up the kitchen and get it ready for the new residents. Tom was reluctant, to say the least, because he had personally known Aunt Sarah and her strict rules about outsiders entering her realm. His protests fell upon deaf ears, however, and Tom, with much trepidation, went into the basement of Lindenwald and entered Aunt Sarah's kitchen. The following is an account of what transpired in Tom's own words:

> "I went down into the cellar and then into the kitchen, but the minute I took up a pan I heard a sound. As I looked up, down the chimney came Aunt Sarah. She was covered with soot, but her eyes were blazing, and the ends of her kerchief stood up on her head just like horns. So I said to myself, 'Tom, you're getting out of this cellar as fast as you can, and nobody's going to make you go back.'"

Perhaps fear and an over-active imagination fueled Tom's sighting, or perhaps Aunt Sarah (who seemed to appear more like a demon-possessed Aunt Jemima) did actually come back to defend her sacred kitchen. While there are no other reports of actual angry Aunt Sarah sightings, a kindlier, gentler Aunt Sarah may have decided to make her presence known in a different manner.

Several families who have occupied Lindenwald have reported waking up in the morning to the smell of buttery, hot pancakes. While strongest in the dining room, the aroma often pervaded the entire house in the early daylight hours. Numerous people searching for the source of this enticing smell have gone down into Sarah's old kitchen, only to find a cold and empty fireplace and griddle. One wonders whether these people were relieved not to find Sarah's ghost cooking phantom pancakes, or were disappointed that the delicious aromas were not to be followed by a hearty breakfast.

While the story of paranormal pancakes sounds farfetched, there was confirmation from a former Supervisory Park Ranger at Lindenwald, Marion Berntson. Apparently, she and others on the staff regularly opened the house early in the morning and were greeted by the delectable, buttery aroma of homemade pancakes! In the face of so many eyewitnesses (or nose-witnesses in this case) over the course of so many generations, we must bow to the inevitable conclusion—Aunt Sarah's pancakes live on!

Berntson also related a story that on one occasion she was locking up the house after the last tour of the day. She thought she was the only one left in the house, until she heard a female voice upstairs. Her immediate thought was that someone had lagged behind or become lost on the tour and was in danger of being locked in for the night. Calling upstairs, she received no response. Still not believing that anything out of the ordinary was going on, she went upstairs to find the lost tourist, but no one was there.

In addition to footsteps, doors closing, and the classic cold spots, Marion Berntson and another Park Ranger encountered a very unusual phenomenon. One New Year's Eve the house was empty and securely locked. In order to preserve the house and its valuable contents, temperature and humidity levels are constantly monitored with equipment known as hydrothermalgraphs. These units produce charts of temperature and humidity twenty-four hours a day. When staff members returned to Lindenwald after the New Year's holiday, they were stunned to find that on midnight of New Year's Eve, the temperature suddenly rose inside the house, almost as if warm-blooded people were partying in the new year. After several hours of this inexplicable spike in tempera ait of Lady Wellington was once over the mantle in one of the rooms at

Lindenwald. Lady Wellington had been a friend of Van Buren's daughter, Angelica, and it was Angelica's portrait that now hung over this mantle. With the assistance of another Park Ranger, Berntson planned to remove Angelica's portrait and replace it with that of Lady Wellington. However, as it was carefully being removed from the wall, Angelica Van Buren's portrait suddenly left their hands and flipped completely around in the air. Startled and perplexed, they decided to put Angelica's portrait back and leave well enough alone.

The National Park system did not acquire Lindenwald until 1976. Prior to that, the home was always in private hands. Some families lived there for decades and heard and saw absolutely nothing unusual. Other families had enough bizarre experiences to fill an entire book.

One such family occupied Lindenwald from the early part of the twentieth century until 1957. Both adults and children alike had many stories to tell of the sounds of footsteps, doors closing, the shutters banging on still nights, unseen figures leaning on their beds, and the phantom strains of violin music playing in an empty room. One of the skeptical men in the family chalked it up all to "women's nerves," until he heard footsteps and promptly left the house in the middle of the night!

Recommendation

Lindenwald is a showpiece of elegance and refinement befitting the home of a former president. Many important and fascinating people have been connected with this place and it is well worth the time to take the forty-five-minute tour to hear the stories of their lives. As there appears to be several former residents still making their presence known in a variety of unique ways, keep your eyes, ears, and nose open on the grounds, the stately rooms of house, and especially Aunt Sarah's kitchen.

Visitor Information
Martin Van Buren National Historic Site
1013 Old Post Road
Kinderhook, New York 12106
www.nps.gov/archive/mava/InfoPark.htm

The Martin Van Buren National Historic Site is open to the public seven days a week from Memorial Day weekend to the end of October. The Site is also open Saturday and Sundays in November through the first week in December. The grounds are open year-round from dawn to dusk. The visitor center is staffed from 9 am until 4:30 pm on days that the park is open. Access to the historic house is by guided tour only. Sign up for tours at the visitor center.

There are a variety of activities throughout the visitor season, including short interpretive talks, bicycle tours, hikes, living history programs, concerts, craft demonstrations, etc.

Call 518-758-9689 for specific activities and dates.

Admission

Adults, (17 years or older), $3 per person. Children, (younger than 17), free. Holders of Golden Eagle, Age or Access Passports, free.

Directions

As listed in their Web site: Martin Van Buren National Historic Site is on New York State Route 9H in Kinderhook, New York.

Approaching from the east on Interstate 90: take exit B1 onto US Route 9 southbound. Bear right onto Route 9H approximately five miles south of Interstate 90. The Site will be on your right in five miles.

Approaching from the west on Interstate 90: take exit 12 onto US Route 9 southbound. Bear right onto Route 9H approximately five miles south of Interstate 90. The Site will be on your right in five miles.

Approaching from the south on Interstate 87 (New York State Thruway): take exit 21 onto NY State Route 23 eastbound across the Rip Van Winkle Bridge (toll). Follow Route 23 for approximately 10 miles. Turn left onto NY State Route 9H northbound. The Site will be on your left in approximately 15 miles.

The Bottom Line

The History: The home of a former president, once owned by the grandfather of Winston Churchill, set in an old Dutch town that inspired Washington Irving to write *The Legend of Sleepy Hollow*. Definitely a top destination in the Hudson Valley for those interested in local and national history, politics, architecture, and decorative arts.

The Haunting: Where else can you possibly glimpse the figure of a former president and a vice-president, catch the aroma of phantom pancakes, while hearing the haunting strains of violin music? Definitely a top destination in the Hudson Valley for those interested in historic haunts.

The Ten Broeck Mansion in Albany.

Ten Broeck Mansion

Abraham Ten Broeck was born into a prominent New York family, and married into another when he wed Elizabeth Van Renssalaer. Ten Broeck was a successful businessman; he led the New York militia at the Battle of Saratoga, had served as mayor of Albany, and by 1797, he was one of the wealthiest men in the city, living in one of the fine townhouses on Broadway.

Unfortunately, a massive fire burned down several blocks of the city that year, including Ten Broeck's house. In need of a new mansion, he had one designed and built in the Federal style at a spot "out in the country" (which is now an urban setting) that afforded a commanding view of the river, hence he named his mansion Prospect.

The Federal style gave way to some Greek Revival alterations in the 1830s, and in 1848 banker Thomas Worth Olcott purchased the house, made some additions and renamed it Arbor Hill. Despite being one the wealthiest and most powerful men in the area, Olcott most enjoyed the simple pleasures of gardening. He also enjoyed giving back to the community to the point where he was once called the "most charitable man in Albany."

The Olcotts lived in the mansion for the next one hundred years, finally donating the house to the Albany County Historical Association. While obtaining such historic treasures is wonderful, maintaining them can be an expensive proposition. By the 1970s, the structure was in need of extensive repairs and association members didn't know where they would get the money to pay for them. Things looked grim, until a door literally opened upon a solution.

For seventy-five years, there was a sealed door in the basement that had never been opened. When association members decided to see what lay behind the door, they were astounded at what they found—an old wine cellar with over 700 bottles of some of the most valuable French wines from 1860s, 70s, and 80s, including cases of Chateau Lafite Rothschild and Chateau Mouton Rothschild. One exuberant wine expert likened the find to the opening of King Tutankhamen's tomb. While that may have been going a bit far, the contents of the wine cellar did fetch a king's ransom, or least enough to finance the restorations and save the historic mansion from crumbling!

> **Note:** To put the value of such rare wine in perspective, one vintage wine Web site currently offers a single bottle of 1870 Chateau Lafite Rothschild for $15,000, or an entire case for $180,000 if you're very thirsty.

The beautiful spiraling staircase in the Ten Broeck Mansion. *Photo by Michael Worden.*

It is known that Dudley Olcott (Thomas' son), along with one of his brothers, purchased many cases of French wines from the Golden Age of wines, which were stored in the basement wine cellar and served at the numerous elaborate dinner parties held at the Mansion. What remains a mystery to this day is why the wine cellar door was sealed for seventy-five years! It is a mystery that may never be solved, but it is a happy twist of fate that ultimately saved the historic house.

There was another odd twist of fate at the Ten Broeck Mansion, but this one falls into the bizarre category. There was a burial vault on the property that contained the remains of the Ten Broecks, and possibly those of General Schuyler, another prominent Albany resident. Sometime in the mid to late nineteenth century, the property was cut into to widen the road. This apparently compromised the foundation of the burial vault, and time and erosion resulted in all of the remains sliding out onto the street! Everyone was quickly reinterred at the Albany Rural Cemetery, although, by that point, it was impossible to tell who had been who.

Perhaps the disturbance to this final resting place stirred things up with the former residents, or perhaps some of them are sticking around simply because they loved the place. Whatever the reason, there have been several unexplained occurrences in the Ten Broeck Mansion in recent years. For example, the haunting strains of a flute have been heard echoing down the empty corridors. In the bedroom on the second floor at the top of the stairs, there is often the feeling that you aren't alone. Some people have claimed to see figures moving about, only to discover no one is there.

In the bedroom where George Washington's portrait is hanging over the mantel, several people have reported witnessing an impression on the pillows and mattress, as if someone was lying down! In that same room, an object placed on the mantel was later found on a nearby chair, even though no one had gone in that room. Fortunately, while such occurrences can be momentarily startling, there has never been anything menacing, and perhaps much of what transpires is just residual memories of times gone by.

Some of the rare vintage wines discovered in the wine cellar that had been sealed for seventy-five years. *Photo by Michael Worden.*

A local psychic has actually conducted séances in the house, and she believes that at least one of the spirits is that of Abraham Ten Broeck. Of course, no one can ever know for sure, but whoever is still walking the corridors, playing the flute, and stretching out on the bed for a nap, must be pleased with the way things have turned out. Thanks to the discovery of a hidden treasure of wine, the mansion was saved and now can be enjoyed for generations to come. That is a story worth telling, and the Ten Broeck Mansion is a place worth visiting.

Recommendation

Of course, you must see the wine cellar in the basement that saved the mansion. There are also some exceptionally fine portraits throughout the house, and the three-story spiral staircase is a thing of beauty. It is also interesting to note that the house has some of the country's oldest bathrooms with indoor plumbing. On the tour, you will learn the stories of the powerful and influential men and women who lived here, wined and dined with presidents and generals, and helped shape the course of the country. And keep an eye on that bed to see if any impressions appear.

Visitor Information

Ten Broeck Mansion
9 Ten Broeck Place
Albany, New York 12210
518-436-9826
www.timesunion.com/communities/tenbroeck

The mansion is open May-December: Thursday and Friday 10 am to 4 pm. Saturday and Sunday 1 pm to 4 pm. January to April by appointment only. School group visits and private tours available all year, and the mansion is available to rent for weddings and special events.

There are numerous programs throughout the season, including Living History the first week in May, a Haunted Mansion in October, Holiday House in December, and summer Archeology Camp for kids. Please call for information and the current calendar of events.

Admission

Adults $5, Seniors and Students $4, Children 12 and under $3, ACHA Members Free.

Directions

As listed in their Web site:

From Interstate 787: Take the Clinton Avenue exit (marked "Downtown Albany") and proceed west on Clinton Avenue. Just past the Palace Theater, turn right onto Ten Broeck Street then proceed north toward Livingston Avenue. Turn left on Ten Broeck Place, and halfway up the hill turn right for the Mansion parking lot.

From Interstate 90: Take Exit 6 (Arbor Hill) and proceed to the traffic light at Livingston Avenue. Turn left onto Livingston Avenue and proceed east. Cross the intersection of North Swan Street and turn right halfway down the hill to the gate for the Ten Broeck Mansion parking lot.

The Bottom Line

The History: Elegant home of the rich and powerful, with a list of family and friends that reads like a *Who's Who* of history, containing many fine works of art and furnishings. Even with all that, one of the most fascinating aspects may be the liquid treasure found in the hidden wine cellar.

The Haunting: The sound of flute music, a bed that gets impressions of someone lying down on it, the feeling of a presence, and figures moving in the bedrooms and halls.

Historic Cherry Hill in Albany. *Photo by Michael Worden.*

Cherry Hill

There may never have been an official aristocracy established in America, but certain families did create powerful dynasties that lacked nothing but the crowns and coronations. In the Hudson Valley, one such family was the Van Rensselaers.

In 1629, Dutch merchant Kiliaen Van Rensselaer (1585-1646) was given a grant for an 850,000-acre tract of land which he called Rensselaerswyck. (Such grants were known as patroonships, and the patroons to whom they were given exercised great power over the land and the people.) This vast area encompassed present-day Albany and the surrounding region, and generations of Van Rennselaer's descendants managed it like feudal lords.

Philip Van Rensselaer, a cousin of the patroon, built his "mansion house," Cherry Hill, in 1787, on a 900-acre farm a mile south of the city of Albany. Cherry Hill was to be the home to five generations of the family. Inevitably, as times changed over the centuries, the family's social prominence and fortunes steadily declined, but they never lost their pride in the Van Rensselaers' once-esteemed position. They were descendants of the first patroon, and they wanted everyone to remember it. In order to preserve that memory, they saved documents, furniture, and everyday objects that ultimately resulted in the preservation of a remarkable 176 years of family history at Cherry Hill.

Ironically, the preservation of all of this material almost destroyed the house itself. With over 30,000 documents and 20,000 objects jammed into the attic, the sheer weight of the family history cracked the walls below and threatened long-term damage to the structure. Fortunately, the last residing family member, Emily Watkinson Rankin, had made provisions for the house to become a museum after her death in 1963, and the heavy stacks of paper and objects were removed and now reside in a separate archive building on the property.

However, while great pains were made to leave a lasting record of the family's history, there was one episode that was given the silent treatment. A scandalous affair and murder took place at Cherry Hill that made national headlines, and for succeeding generations the event became the official skeleton in the family closet. Fortunately for us, it was well documented at the time and now provides a fascinating glimpse into the lives and loves of a prominent New York family.

The year was 1826, and a Van Rensselaer cousin, Mrs. Elsie Lansing Whipple, and her husband, John, were living with the family at Cherry Hill. Married at fourteen, Elsie was from a prominent Albany family and had inherited considerable money and property. Economically and socially, it was an advantageous match for John. He was often away on business, and when a charming man, Jesse Strang, came to be employed by the family, there was an instant attraction and the wheel of fate was set into motion.

The ingredients for a crime were all there: a possible loveless marriage, a twenty-five-year-old bored housewife with a roving eye, a young man consumed by passion, and a lot of money at stake. According to Jesse's confession, it was Elsie who first hatched the plot to poison her husband so that she and Jesse could run away together and start a new life in Ohio. When arsenic failed to do the job, Jesse claimed she coerced him to climb outside her husband's window and shoot him in May of 1827.

According to Jesse Strang, it was all remarkably well planned, and had the two kept their silence, it might have had a different outcome. However, Elsie quickly admitted to the affair and Jesse eventually confessed to the shooting after a month of being in jail and undergoing exhausting interrogations. At that point, justice should have been served, but social standing still had its privileges.

Jesse Strang was convicted, in part, due to the testimony of a recently-freed family slave, Dinah Johnson, who claimed that Jesse had offered her $500 to poison Whipple, and he was executed in Albany's last public hanging. The event drew huge crowds, with people traveling great distances to witness the gruesome spectacle.

Elsie's fate was altogether different. She never admitted to any part of the murder plot, and Jesse was not allowed to testify against her! His confession was extremely detailed and very compelling, but the jury was not to hear a word of it. With no hard evidence and no witnesses who corroborated his version of the events, Elsie was acquitted. She quickly left Albany to escape the universal scorn and scandal, and died just a few years later.

So, who was the spider and who was the fly in this case? As Elsie never confessed to anything more than an affair, we only have Jesse's side of the story. Was his account honest and accurate, and had it actually been Elsie who seduced him into murdering her husband? Or, had the clever hired hand seen a way to manipulate a foolish young woman and get his hands on her fortune by eliminating the one person in his way?

No one will ever know for sure, but if ever there was a recipe for a crime, and a haunting, it's contained in the events surrounding the 1827 murder. Historian and popular folklorist Louis Jones wrote that the murder had created a restless spirit at Cherry Hill, although the legend doesn't state who once belonged to that spirit—the victim, John Whipple, his convicted murderer, Jesse Strang, or the unfaithful wife, Elsie, who may have returned out of guilt for causing the death of two men. As we can never truly know what is in the hearts and minds of the living, so, too, are ghosts often a mystery that may never be solved.

One thing is for certain, love leaves an indelible mark, for better and for worse. The Van Rensselaer family loved their heritage and their home, and preserved an astounding wealth of documents and objects for future generations to enjoy and study.

Elsie and Jesse may have truly loved one another, but their unbridled passion led to death and destruction. Still, some noble sentiments did arise from the terrible events, even as Jesse faced his own execution. In his lengthy written confession, in regards to Elsie he concluded, "And for the love I once entertained for her, I do rejoice that she has been acquitted. And I do most fervently pray, that she will devote the remainder of her life, to sincere contrition and repentance, and that she may, above all things, enjoy everlasting peace, consolation and happiness in heaven."

Recommendation

Cherry Hill is so much more than a historic home with a collection of furniture, paintings, and papers. It is a place that offers a unique glimpse into the lives of five generations of an important New York family. The current interpretation of the house is the story of the family from 1884-1963, and the vast document collection is available for research by appointment.

Then there is the 1827 murder. Much like the later famous murder trial of Lizzie Borden, but with even more salacious details, the affair, murder, trial, and execution read like a spellbinding novel. A fascinating way to experience Cherry Hill is to attend one of their special murder investigation tours where you get an in-depth look at the case at the actual scene of the crime.

Visitor Information

Historic Cherry Hill
523 1/2 South Pearl Street
Albany, New York 12202
518-434-4791
info@historiccherryhill.org
www.historiccherryhill.org/index.htm

Hours

Historic Cherry Hill is open to visitors from April through December. April-June, tours are on the hour: Tuesday to Friday 12-3, Saturday 10-3, Sunday 1-3. July-September, tours: Tuesday to Saturday tours 10-3, Sunday 1-3. October to December, tours: Tuesday-Friday 12-3, Saturday 10-3, Sunday, 1-3. Closed January through March, Mondays, and major holidays.

A variety of programs are offered for all ages, including tours and school programs, special events and murder investigation tours.

Admission

$5 for adults, $4 for senior citizens and college students, $2 for children 6-17

Groups of ten or more require advance reservations. Special admission rates are available for groups. Group tours can be arranged by calling or writing the museum. Specially designed tours for school children and youth groups are available by advance reservation. Special admission rates apply.

There is a museum shop featuring books, note papers, cards, and museum reproductions. Museum admission is not required to visit the shop.

Directions

From their Web site: Historic Cherry Hill is located at 523 1/2 South Pearl Street in Albany, just off Exit 2 of Interstate 787. From the North, take Exit 2. At the light, turn left, and look for Historic Cherry Hill immediately on your right. From the South, take exit 2, and follow the ramp straight to the end. At the light turn left. Under the overpass, take another left onto Route 32 South. Bear right onto 787's exit ramp. At the light, turn left, and look for Historic Cherry Hill immediately on your right.

The Bottom Line

The History: The home, furnishings, and documents of 176 years of the Van Rensselaers offering an in-depth look into five generations of an important New York family. The scandalous murder case of 1827 provides a fascinating glimpse into a timeless crime of passion set in an earlier era when the law did not treat everyone fairly (which is probably also not so different from today).

The Haunting: Popular folklorist Louis Jones wrote that the murder created a restless spirit at Cherry Hill, but to whom does the spirit belong?

The Canfield Casino in Congress Park, Saratoga Springs. The building now houses the Saratoga Springs History Museum.

Canfield Casino in Congress Park

A typical town may have a small park on the main street with a bandstand that has seen better days, a statue of some half-forgotten founder, or an old cannon with a cement-filled barrel that has become more of a climbing toy for kids than a war memorial.

However, Saratoga Springs is not a typical town, and Congress Park is by no means your average park. Located downtown on Broadway, entering the park is reminiscent of walking onto the grounds of an elegant European estate. Like temples to some deity, there are the columned structures housing the Congress and Columbian Springs, there are duck ponds, statuary, and an antique carousel for kids or those still kids at heart.

The centerpiece of the park, however, is the impressive former casino, built in 1870 to lighten the bulging bankrolls of high rolling tourists. It was the creation of John Morrissey, a champion prize fighter turned Congressman, who no doubt learned a thing or two about gambling from both professions. In 1894, Richard Canfield bought the casino and ran a very successful operation until the anti-gambling populace and government shut the doors in 1907.

However, the gamblers' loss turned out to be history's gain, as the building now houses the Saratoga Springs History Museum. The museum has three floors of exhibits, but the building itself is a sight to see with its huge rooms and towering ceilings. And if you've ever wanted to breathe the rarified air of a high-stakes gambling parlor, the museum has preserved some of the casino's original furniture and gaming equipment in a room where men with big cigars and bigger bank accounts used to wager hundreds of thousands of dollars in an age when the average worker was lucky to make $500 a year.

It is by the roulette table in this room where the figure of one of the old casino's former gamblers is still seen today. Could this man have lost his fortune on this table, and is still trying to recover it? Or is he simply trying to reconnect with happier times in life when money and champagne flowed freely?

There is another figure from a time gone by that walks the halls of the Canfield Casino—a blond woman in a Victorian-era dress. As the casino never permitted women, what could her spirit be doing here? Perhaps when some antiques were brought into the museum to put on display, she came along with a favorite item from her past.

In addition to these two figures, there have also been numerous reports of voices, cigar smoke, and other inexplicable occurrences throughout the building. Passersby have also noted lights going on and off and shades going up and down when the building is closed and empty.

While it may be unusual for the average museum to have such things going on, just remember that Saratoga Springs is not your average place. And it is somehow fitting that in a building that strives to give glimpses into the past, these spirits may be doing that quite literally—and that's a possibility you shouldn't bet against.

The temple-like structures in Congress Park which house
the mineral springs.

The roulette table where the figure of a man is seen trying to place a bet. *Photo by Dr. Art Donohue.*

Recommendation

Whatever amount of time you have allotted for the Canfield Casino, double it so you can also enjoy a stroll through the park to see the gardens, ponds, and springs.

Visitor Information

The Saratoga Springs History Museum
P. O. Box 216
1 East Congress Street
The Canfield Casino in Congress Park
Saratoga Springs, New York 12866
(518) 584-6920, (518) 581-1477 fax
www.saratogahistory.org

The museum is open daily Memorial Day through Labor Day, 10am – 4pm.

Closed Monday and Tuesday the remainder of the year.

There are tours, lectures, and special events throughout the year for adults and children. Go to their Web site or call for information on these events. For information on renting the Canfield Casino, call (518) 587-3550 x471

Admission

$5 Adults, $4 Seniors and Students, Children Under 12 Admitted Free

Directions

From the South: New York State Thruway to Exit 24 onto I-87 North to Exit 13N (Route 9). Drive north on Route 9 approximately 4 miles. Route 9 is Broadway in Saratoga Springs. Congress Park is on your right, by the intersection of Broadway and Congress Street.

From the North: I-87 South to Exit 15. Make right turn off ramp and travel 3 miles to intersection making a left turn onto Broadway (at The Prime Hotel) then travel one mile south. Congress Park is on your left, by the intersection of Broadway and Congress Street.

The Bottom Line

The History: It's wonderful to drive or walk through the town and see the magnificent old houses, but to really understand and appreciate the people and the way they lived 100 years ago, this museum provides that insight with photos, furnishings, etc., in the magnificent setting of a casino built in 1870.

The Haunting: A man is seen by the roulette table and a woman in a Victorian dress is seen walking the halls. There are numerous reports of inexplicable sights, sounds, and smells.

The Inn at Saratoga.

Inn at Saratoga

Many hotels have come and gone in Saratoga Springs, but the Inn at Saratoga claims the honor of being the oldest continuously-operated hotel in town. Opening its doors in 1843 as a boarding house to accommodate the growing influx of tourists arriving for the spring waters, the inn has undergone many changes with an eclectic variety of owners.

In 1846, Dr. Richard Allen provided his guests/patients who stayed at the inn with supervised diets as part of his treatments that utilized the waters that were thought to have medicinal properties. In 1866, another owner added the large, three-story addition to the rear. At one point in its history, a walkway connected the main building to yet another addition, bringing the total number of rooms to over 200.

It was Primo Suarez (for whom the current restaurant at the inn is named) who created the Victorian façade in 1887. He operated the inn as a destination for Cuban tourists. The place catered to a Jewish clientele from the 1920s to 1973 when it was operated by a rabbi and his family.

Today, the inn has thirty-eight rooms and four luxury cottages, and strives to provide a refined Victorian experience for tourists interested in the wide variety of arts and entertainment available in the area. With such a long and colorful history, does the inn also have something to offer guests who are looking for an experience a little out of the ordinary, say for example, a ghost or two? In fact it does, and many employees will attest to experiencing inexplicable sights and sounds.

It appears as if the third floor is the most active, and, over the years, some of the housekeepers have reported seeing figures, hearing voices, and having doors opening and closing. A desk clerk had a particularly interesting encounter one day when she entered the elevator on the third floor and pushed the button to go down to the first floor. The elevator door started to close, then stopped half way and opened again. Thinking a guest also wanted to go down, she expected to see someone else get in the elevator.

Seconds passed and no one else entered, and she looked out into the hall and saw no one, so she pushed the button to close the door. Again the elevator door stopped half way, and opened again. Once more she checked the hallway, then tried a third, and then a fourth time to get the doors to close. As she waited, she suddenly felt a shift in the weight of the elevator, as if an adult had just stepped into it on the other side. The doors finally closed, and on the short ride to the first floor—which seemed very long that day—she distinctly heard what sounded like someone impatiently drumming their fingers on the wall of the elevator. Needless to say, she was quite relieved to get out of the elevator and away from that particular "guest."

Employees often hear voices, particularly on the basement level. When the desk clerk went to the basement to find the maintenance man one day, she clearly heard a male voice, and assuming it was the maintenance man, called his name. There was no response, so she went down the hall and checked every room, finding no one. When she reached the end of hall, she then clearly heard a female voice behind her. Again, she checked every room, to no avail. Later, she discovered that the maintenance man was not even in the building at the time.

Most recently, one housekeeper had a startling experience. It's standard practice to prop open the door to a room with the garbage can when it's being cleaned. This day, the woman put the can against the open door as she had hundreds of times before. When she turned for a moment to get something off her cart, the door slammed shut with such force it propelled the garbage can and its contents into the hall.

She reported the incident to management, but no one was able to find a rational explanation. No windows were open, and when the door was opened and let go, it slowly moved but didn't even have enough force to close and latch, let alone slam shut and propel a garbage can.

There are also many sightings in the lobby. Employees will glimpse someone passing through or approaching the desk, only to look up and find no one there. They have checked to see if passing car headlights or reflections are the cause, but here again, no rational reasons have been found to explain the appearances of the phantom guests.

With over a century and a half of people seeking cures, gamblers betting on the races, or simple tourists looking for a break in their everyday routines, the Inn at Saratoga has no doubt seen its share of human drama. Have some of its former guests neglected to check out? You'll just have to stay a while and find out for yourself.

Recommendation

The Inn at Saratoga provides an excellent central location from which to explore the town on foot, and their breakfast buffet will give you the energy to do so. And if you are too tired to go out after a long day of sightseeing, the Inn's restaurant, Primo's, offers "informal fine dining" seven days a week. Request a room on the third floor if you want the best chance of having an unusual encounter.

Visitor Information

Inn at Saratoga
231 Broadway
Saratoga Springs, New York 12866
(518) 583-1890
info@theinnatsaratoga.com
www.theinnatsaratoga.com

Call or check their Web site for rates and reservations, or to book a special event.

Directions

As listed on their Web site:

From the South: New York State Thruway to Exit 24 onto I-87 North to Exit 13N (Route 9). Drive north on Route 9 approximately 4 miles. Route 9 is Broadway in Saratoga Springs. The Inn at Saratoga is on the left, at the corner of Broadway and Circular Streets.

From the North: I-87 South to Exit 15. Make right turn off ramp and travel 3 miles to intersection making a left turn onto Broadway (at The Prime Hotel) then travel one mile south. The Inn at Saratoga is on the right, at the corner of Broadway and Circular Streets.

From the West: New York State Thruway to Exit 27 - Amsterdam. After the Toll Booth take your first right turn. Follow Route 67 East signs through the City of Amsterdam. Head East approximately 20 miles into Ballston Spa, at the light you take a left turn onto Route 50 North. Route 50 North will bring you right into Saratoga Springs. Route 50 will intersect with Broadway (Route 9). At the light, make a left turn and the Inn at Saratoga is on the left.

From the East: Take Route 90 (Mass Turnpike to the NYS Thruway), then exit the Thruway onto Exit 787 North. Take 787 North to Exit for Route 7 West. Take Route 7 West until you get to 87 North Exit (Adirondack Northway). Follow the Northway to the Saratoga Springs Exit 13 North. You may then follow the directions From the South.

The Bottom Line

The History: The oldest continually-operated hotel in Saratoga Springs, opening its doors back in 1843. The Inn has hosted guests who came for the medicinal waters, Cuban and Jewish tourists, people coming for the races, the arts center, and those simply looking for fresh air.

The Haunting: The third floor appears to be the most active. Figures are seen, voices are heard, and doors open and close on their own.

> *Time is*
> *Too slow for those who wait*
> *Too swift for those who fear*
> *Too long for those who grieve*
> *Too short for those who rejoice*
> *But for those who Love Time is*
> *Eternity*
>
> ~Henry Van Dyke

This poem, by Henry Van Dyke, is inscribed on the sundial that rests on a marble table at the center of the magnificent Yaddo Gardens in Saratoga Springs, New York. The sentiments about love expressed in this poem reflect upon the very existence of the gardens—created out of the love a man had for his wife, memorializing the loss of beloved children, and ultimately its dedication to the arts that the owners so much admired and loved.

Yaddo Gardens

Yaddo Gardens in Saratoga Springs.

Yaddo began as a private estate for a wealthy Wall Street stockbroker, Spencer Trask. After spending several happy summers in the area, in 1881, he purchased 400 acres in order to build an idyllic retreat for his wife, Katrina, and their children. Unfortunately, there would be little joy for this family, as tragedy after tragedy struck with fatal blows.

Before moving into the Queen Anne style house Trask had built, one of their sons died. Several years later, Katrina Trask was presumed to be fatally ill with diphtheria. Ignorant of the deadly contagious nature of the disease, their daughter and son kissed her goodbye. It would literally be a kiss of death, as Katrina survived, while both children contracted diphtheria and rapidly succumbed. The Trasks had a fourth child the next year, but she did not live even two weeks.

For most people, the final blow to Yaddo would have been when the Trask's house burned down. However, instead of abandoning the scene of so much tragedy, they decided not to give into their grief and create an even more impressive home—the fifty-five-room mansion that today still stands like a majestic, fairytale castle. However, this would be one fairytale that would not have a happy ending.

In 1909, Spencer Trask was killed in a train accident while returning to Yaddo from his business in New York City. Katrina had now lost her entire family, but there was one thing for her to hold onto—the dream that she and Spencer had about creating an artist colony at Yaddo. That dream finally came true in 1926, when the first artists arrived. Many decades later, Yaddo continues to host prize-winning writers, composers, painters, sculptors, and artists in all fields in their residency programs.

The sundial that has the Van Dyke poem.

How many artists have been inspired by the Italianate garden at Yaddo, with its roses, fountains, and sculptures? It's impossible to say, but in a town that bustles with tourists and racing fans, the garden that Spencer designed for his wife is a haven of serenity.

Could the Yaddo Mansion and its garden also be a haven of another sort, as well? Could more than artists be in residence? If we are to believe the several eyewitness accounts, Katrina Trask still walks the halls of her former home. She has clearly been seen wearing a Victorian dress, looking every inch the former mistress of the house. Perhaps she returns because she is pleased with how her plans have come to fruition?

While the mansion is not open to the public, the gardens are, so travelers looking for an unusual experience will not be disappointed as there appears to be apparitions among the many flowers. Strange lights have been photographed in the gardens, specifically in the rose garden at the southwest corner. An odd whistling sound has also been heard on the premises for several decades, and no source has ever been found.

What spirits walk the gardens and mansion at Yaddo? Gentle ones, to be sure. Whether drawn by the beauty of the place, or somehow connected to the many tragedies that befell the Trasks, Yaddo continues to prove that love can indeed triumph over tragedy, and like the human spirit, endures.

Recommendation

The gardens are probably best enjoyed when the roses are in bloom, but they are worth a pleasant stroll at any time of the year. There is also a rock garden that contains a variety of flowers that bloom at various times of the season. Note the "ST/KT" (Spencer Trask/Katrina Trask) on the entrance gate, look for the statue dedicated to the Trask children, and read the inscription on the sundial. Again, the mansion is not open to the public, so please respect their privacy.

Visitor Information

Yaddo Gardens
Route 9P (Union Avenue)
Saratoga Springs, New York
(518) 584-0746
http://yaddo.org/garden/home.asp

Yaddo Gardens are open every day from 8 am to dusk.

Admission

The gardens are free of charge to the public. There is a $5 fee for guided tours that are offered on the following schedule:

Saturdays and Sundays beginning from mid-June through early September. During the Saratoga Race Course season (late July through Labor Day), guided tours also are offered on Tuesdays. All guided tours begin at 11 am and start near the large fountain at the entrance to the gardens. The tours include historical information about Yaddo.

Directions

As listed on their Web site:

From the City of Saratoga Springs: Proceed east from the center of the city on Union Avenue (NY Route 9P). Just after you pass the NYRA Thoroughbred race track you will come to a stoplight. Turn right at the light and follow the signs to the gardens bearing left as you go.

From all other areas: Travel Interstate 87 to Exit 14 in Saratoga Springs. Turn right on NY Route 9P North. At the first stoplight, turn left into Yaddo and follow the signs to the gardens bearing left as you go.

The Bottom Line

The History: A poignant story of a wealthy family who lost their children, but from that tragedy created a prize-winning artist colony.

The Haunting: Mrs. Trask has been seen walking through the mansion. Strange lights have been photographed in the gardens, and an inexplicable whistling sound is heard on the grounds.

In its history, the town of Athens has had ice houses, brick yards, a cotton mill, a machine shop, and pottery manufacturers. First and foremost, however, it has had the Hudson River, and with the advent of ship building and the ferry service, Athens really put itself on the map. Until the building of the Rip Van Winkle Bridge in 1935, the life's blood of the town was the Athens-Hudson (the town across the river) ferry, as well as the steamships that plied the waters between Albany and New York City.

There is the old proverb about those who live by the sword, die by the sword, and unfortunately such was the case in Athens—both literally, and figuratively. When the bridge opened, ferries became obsolete and the local businesses began to slowly die off. However, a century earlier, there was a far more tragic ship-related event.

It was commonplace for steamship captains to race one another, and on April 7, 1845, the *Swallow* was engaged in a friendly competition with the *Rochester* and the *Express* on their way from Albany to New York City. A sudden fierce snow squall severely diminished visibility and the *Swallow* steamed right into the small, rocky Dooper's Island off the coast of Athens. The ship struck with such force, it broke in two and burst into flames. Despite the best efforts of the people of Athens to rescue survivors from the icy water, it is estimated that as many as forty people drown right in front of the town. Some victims were probably no more than a few yards from shore, but the snow was so intense they didn't know which way to swim to land.

Did so many tragic deaths leave an imprint on Athens? Possibly, as local residents claim that many places in town have restless spirits. Perhaps the most well known is the Stewart House, which is literally a stone's throw from the Hudson River. The place was built in 1883 as a hotel to accommodate all the tourists and businessmen, and it became *the* place to be when in Athens.

Hardy Stewart was so proud of his new establishment, he had his name set in iron at the main entrance. Unfortunately, as skilled as the iron worker was in his craft, he was most likely illiterate, as the large letters prominently displaying the name of Stewart for all to see contains a backward "S"! The current owner, Owen Lipstein, has decided to accentuate this quirk, and has incorporated the misdirected letter into all the logos on the restaurant, the tables, the menus, and it has even been set into the bricks by the garden pavilion.

Many famous people have stayed here throughout the hotel's history. Movie buffs will also be interested to know that Meryl Streep "died" in one of the bedrooms in the movie *Iron Weed*, and Dakota Fanning stayed

The Stewart House in Athens.

Stewart House

The ironworker's mistake—the backward "S" at Stewart's entrance.

here while filming part of Steven Spielberg's *War of the Worlds*. (Spielberg also gave high praise to the Stewart House's restaurant.)

With so many people who have come and gone in the past century, it would be difficult to pinpoint what spirits might still be walking the halls of the Stewart House, opening and closing its doors, and making their voices echo down the corridors in the dead of night, but Hardy Stewart may be a candidate. One of the more common occurrences is the sound of someone walking up to a door fumbling for his keys. This is a very distinctive sound, and not like the sound of modern keys, which could be a clue as to the time period of the spirit. These keys clanking together sound like old fashioned skeleton keys, and they are most often heard around closing time. Perhaps Hardy is still following his old habits?

There is other inexplicable activity in the Stewart House involving keys—they disappear. One day, a member of the staff affixed numbered tags to each of the keys for the nine guest rooms and hung them on a board. A short time later, she noticed that the key to room #2 was missing. There was another woman in the building that day, but she insisted she didn't have any reason to take the key and had no idea what happened to it.

Two days of searching produced no results, and finally a locksmith was called. The locksmith arrived, and as the woman began to tell him what was needed, she noticed that suddenly there was key #2 hanging in its proper place!

Of course, this could have been a prank of the living variety, but consider this—keys have disappeared when no one else was in the building, and have even gone missing from people's pockets. Generally, they reappear in odd places about two days later. There have also been witnesses to objects moving on their own, as in the case of one employee who walked into a room and suddenly all the containers on a shelf were pushed off, as if someone pushed them in a sweeping arm motion.

There are many other ghost stories here, perhaps a century of stories. Stay at the Stewart House, or dine here, and see which shades of the past reveal themselves to you.

Recommendation

For a complete experience, stay in one of the guest bedrooms, many of which have beautiful river views. (The river is right across the street.) The restaurant gets top reviews, and you can sip an after dinner drink in the garden pavilion and just watch the river roll by. Look for the backward *S* on the doorstep, and see how many others you can find. Make sure you take a look at the tin ceilings and wall murals in both the bar and dining room. Movie buffs can ask for rooms where actors have stayed. (And don't forget to hang onto your keys!)

Visitor Information

Stewart House
2 North Water Street
Athens, New York 12015
Restaurant: 518-945-1357; Open Wed-Sun 5 to 10 pm
Inn: 518-945-1333

Directions

From the New York State Thruway Northbound: Take exit 21 toward S. Cairo/Cairo, and merge onto CR-23B. Right onto Forrest Hills Avenue. Turn right at Leeds Athens Road. In 3.7 miles turn right onto 2nd Street and in 0.5 miles turn left on North Water Street. Stewart House will be on your left.

From the New York State Thruway Southbound: Take exit 21B for US-9W S toward Coxsackie/RT 81. Turn left on US-9W. In 7.4 miles, turn left onto CR-28/Schoharie Turnpike. In 2.8 miles, turn left at 2nd Street and in 0.5 miles turn left onto North Water Street.

The Bottom Line

The History: In 1845 a steamship was wrecked off Athens. In 1883, the Stewart House was built and has operated as a hotel and restaurant where many famous people (including movie stars) have stayed and dined.

The Haunting: Footsteps, voices, objects moving, and keys regularly disappear.

> *O Cedar Grove! when'er I think to part*
> *From thine all peaceful shades my aching heart*
> *Is like to his who leaves some blessed shore*
> *A weeping exile ne'er to see it more.*
> ~Thomas Cole, 1834

Cedar Grove, the home of Thomas Cole in Catskill.

Cedar Grove:
The Thomas Cole House

To be sure, Thomas Cole loved this house and the beautiful views of the Catskill Mountains to the west. However, his legacy is far greater than his poetry—Cole was, in fact, the founder of the Hudson River School of Art, which was the very first true American genre of painting.

Cole was born in England in 1801, and came to the United States in 1818. It was love at first sight when he visited the Catskill Mountains in 1825, and despite his world travels, he was inexorably drawn back to the area's magnificent vistas, and ultimately chose to make Cedar Grove his home.

Unlike many artists, Cole's talents were recognized early in life and he was made a fellow of the National Academy while only in his twenties. His paintings of the region were hauntingly romantic, and his style started a wave of such landscapes by many different artists, which collectively came to be known as the Hudson River School.

Cole first rented a building at Cedar Grove in 1832 and established a studio. In 1836, he married the owner's niece, Mariah, and took up residence in the main house, which is a fine example of Federal architecture built in 1815. As Cole's fame grew, Cedar Grove became host to many great painters and literary figures of the time, such as James Fenimore Cooper.

Thomas Cole appeared to be destined to become one of the country's most distinguished and accomplished men, until a sudden illness struck him down.

After attending church service one cold Sunday morning in February of 1848, he began feeling tired and weak. Diagnosed with pleurisy and congestion of the lungs, Cole quickly became gravely ill. On Friday, he passed away in his beloved home at the age of just forty-seven.

In Cole's poem, he wrote about how his heart ached at the thought of never again seeing Cedar Grove, but perhaps he needn't have worried about death separating him from this place. There have been several eyewitness reports from employees and docents claiming to have seen and heard things that indicate the great artist may still be in residence.

One of the docents at Cedar Grove is also an artist, and one day she was on the side porch working on a painting. She was looking towards the west at the mountains, when suddenly she saw something in a nearby window. Looking more closely, she clearly saw Thomas Cole dressed in a suit, with his wife in a long dress standing next to him. They were both just looking out the window as if admiring the view.

This could not have been a case of someone playing a practical joke, because the room where the couple was standing, known as the Museum Room, is kept locked and no one was inside. The docent has been described as a very reliable and honest person, and certainly not prone to seeing things. She's reluctant to say she saw a ghost, but insists she saw Cole and his wife standing there as plain as day.

One afternoon, an employee went down to the lower level to use the restroom. On the floor above her, she heard more than one person walking around, and then heard muffled voices as if they were having a conversation. She came back upstairs to see who was there, and found no one. And that wouldn't be the only time she heard the footsteps and voices—on several other occasions when she was alone in the house she has heard these people walking and talking.

Several years ago, a woman on one of the tours announced that she was psychic and had seen Thomas Cole in his studio, as well as his wife in the house with the children. Another visitor had a fascinating experience when she entered the west parlor. A warm feeling swept over her and she actually hugged herself and smiled. She couldn't explain the wonderful sensation, and hadn't experienced it anywhere

The view to the west from the front porch of Cole's beloved Catskill Mountains.

else in the house or on the property. The west parlor was where Cole and Mariah had been married, perhaps she sensed some of that happy experience?

If Thomas Cole couldn't bear to leave Cedar Grove, who could blame him? The Catskill Mountains held a powerful attraction for him in life, so perhaps their beauty still captivates him to this day. At the very least, his magnificent paintings live on so that he can share his love of the Hudson Valley with generations to come.

Recommendation

You don't need to be an art historian to appreciate this place. The house, grounds, and scenery are beautiful in any season. Everything is extraordinarily well documented, even to the receipt for the stately honey locust tree planted in front of the porch in 1817. The staff is extremely knowledgeable and the forty-minute tour is well worth the time.

Visitor Information

Cedar Grove, The Thomas Cole National Historic Site
218 Spring Street
Catskill, New York 12414
518-943-7465
www.thomascole.org

Admission

Admission to the Main House and Old Studio is by guided tour. Tickets are $7 per person during regular open hours. Seniors and students with ID are $5 per person. Tickets are sold in the Visitor Center. Admission to the grounds is free of charge.

Hours

The Main House and Studio are open by guided tour. From the first Saturday in May through the last Sunday in October, tours are offered Thursday, Friday, Saturday & Sunday 10 am to 4 pm. (Please note: The last tour begins at 3 pm.) Tours are offered at other times by appointment.

Tours

Tours of the Main House begin approximately every hour on a first-come-first-served basis. Tours last about forty minutes, and each tour is limited to approximately twelve people. Group Tours are welcome by advance appointment by calling 518-943-7465 or use their online form.

Directions

As listed on their Web site:

From NYC & Points South: Take NYS Thruway (I-87) to exit 21 (Catskill). Make a left at the traffic light, then proceed 1,000 feet and make a left onto Route 23 East. Proceed 2 miles and make a right at the light onto Spring Street (Route 385). Cedar Grove is on the left, (use the shared driveway with Temple Israel).

From Albany & Points North: Take NYS Thruway (I-87) to exit 21 (Catskill). Make a left at the traffic light, then proceed 1,000 feet and make a left onto Route 23 East. Proceed 2 miles and make a right at the light onto Spring Street (Route 385). Cedar Grove is on the left, (use the shared driveway with Temple Israel).

From Points West: Take Route 23 East two miles East of the NYS Thruway exit, make a right at the light onto Spring Street (Route 385) Cedar Grove is on the left (use the shared driveway with Temple Israel).

From Points East: Take the Massachusetts Turnpike to the NYS Thruway (Route 90 West) to exit 2B (Taconic Parkway) Take Taconic Parkway South to Route 23 West. Continue on Route 23

West and cross the Hudson River over The Rip Van Winkle bridge. Make a left at the first light at the intersection of Route 23 and Route 385 (Spring Street). Cedar Grove is on the left (use the shared driveway with Temple Israel).

Or:

Take the Taconic Parkway North to the Hudson Exit (Route 82 North) to Route 23 West. (Note: Route 82 also crosses the Taconic further south. Do not take Route 82 until you see the sign for Hudson.) Cross the Hudson River over The Rip Van Winkle bridge. Make a left at the first light at the intersection of Route 23 and Route 385 (Spring Street). Cedar Grove is on the left (use the shared driveway with Temple Israel).

The Bottom Line

The History: Cedar Grove is not only beautiful, it has great historical significance for the art world and the Hudson Valley. It is one of the most important restorations in New York. Thomas Cole was the founder of the Hudson River School of Art, which was the first truly American art movement.

The Haunting: Thomas Cole and his wife are still seen, and there are footsteps and muffled voices heard in the house.

Section Two

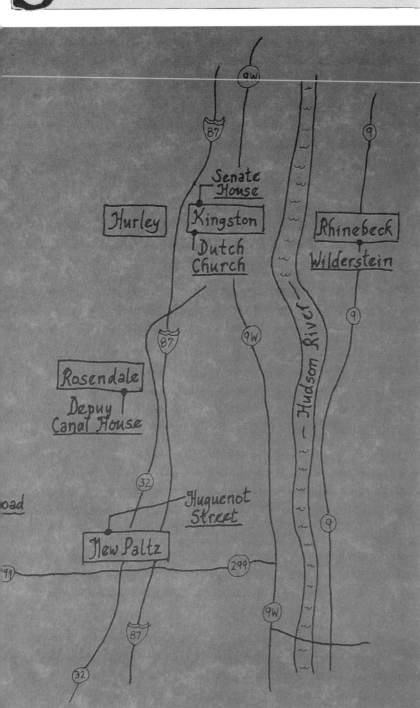

Wilderstein

There is something very different about this place. While it is an imposing landmark standing regally amongst forty landscaped acres with stunning views of the Hudson River, handfuls of mansions can claim those qualities.

No, what's delightfully different about Wilderstein is that there is a remarkable personal quality that gives you the sense of being invited into someone's home, not just visiting a cold, sterile museum. Also, because the house is basically just as it was the day the last owner died, you feel as though the family just went out for a walk and they'll be back shortly.

If you had dropped by when the last owner, the enigmatic Margaret "Daisy" Suckley, was still alive, she no doubt would have asked you to join her on the veranda for a cup of tea. She then would have regaled you with stories about the golden years of Wilderstein and the multitude of family and friends who passed many happy hours here. Daisy might also have told you that she had been a close friend of Franklin D. Roosevelt, and that it was she who had given him his famous Scottish Terrier, Fala.

The story of the location of Wilderstein goes back at least to the time when Native Americans thought this spot was significant enough to carve a rare petroglyph on a large rock near the riverbank. The petroglyph depicts a man wearing a headdress with three feathers, holding a peace pipe in one hand and a tomahawk (this part of the image has since eroded away) in the other—a very interesting combination of images. Did it symbolize a chief who preferred peace, but was prepared for war, or was it a man determined to impose his brand of peace at the end of a tomahawk?

There is speculation that the image depicts Chief Ankony, who ceded the land to the Dutch in 1628, but without supporting evidence there's no telling how many centuries the petroglyph has kept watch on this land. Whatever the origin, its legacy is that this "wild man's stone" is responsible for the name of the estate, Wilderstein.

Much of Wilderstein has been beautifully restored to its original glory, but some sections, such as these stairs and window, still show the years of neglect.

When Thomas Holy Suckley purchased the property in 1852, it was a simple sheep meadow of an adjoining estate. His father had made his fortune in import/export and in real estate, and as one of the heirs to this fortune, Thomas decided that when he married, he would settle down on a country estate. The Suckleys were no strangers to the region, however, as the branches of their family tree read like a *Who's Who* of Hudson Valley history—with names such as Montgomery, Beekman, Livingston, and Van Renssalaer.

The original home was a relatively small, two-story Italianate villa. However, when Thomas' son Robert Bowne Suckley inherited the house in 1888, he completely transformed the structure into a large three-story Queen Anne mansion with a lovely veranda and a five story circular tower. The interior designer was Joseph Burr Tiffany (Louis Comfort Tiffany's cousin) and the landscaping was the work of Calvert Vaux, who co-designed New York City's Central Park. It all combined into a prime example of that simple equation: Money + Talent/Good Taste = Magnificent Estate.

Unfortunately, such a place required a staff of a few dozen maids, butlers, gardeners, and stable boys, and when hard times hit, Robert decided to close up the expensive house and move his family to Switzerland. Ten years later they returned, and despite the eventual loss of the family fortune, Daisy was to live the rest of her long 100 year life there, making the best she could of her grand surroundings under greatly diminished circumstances.

Daisy was always perceived to be a prim and proper spinster, and although she spent a lot of time with FDR, no one ever suspected that it was anything more than a peripheral friendship. However, after Daisy's death in 1991, an old suitcase was found under her bed. It contained a treasure trove of letters between Daisy and FDR, clearly indicating that their private relationship was something far deeper than anyone imagined. While details of a possible affair were not spelled out, it became obvious that Daisy had carried a very big secret to her grave.

Prior to her death, she arranged for the property, house, and contents to go to the Wilderstein Preservation organization so that everything she had known and loved wouldn't crumble beneath the wrecking ball. As the house had fallen into disrepair from decades of neglect, the task of restoration and preservation has been an enormous one. However, with the challenges come great rewards, as the house is something of an historic time capsule containing thousands of letters, photographs, articles of clothing, and everyday objects. It is a site unlike most others because it is still very much a work in progress and with so many potential discoveries waiting to be made, the fascinating story of Wilderstein cannot yet have its final chapter written.

Recent years have seen the exterior undergoing restoration and getting its first coat of paint in seventy-five years, although at the time of the writing of this book, a section of the house still has its gloomy, exposed, dark wooden surface. The entrance and dining room are lined with rich mahogany panels that immediately speak to the former wealth of the Suckley family. And if that doesn't impress you, behold the visages of the family matriarchs in the portraits along the hallway, reminding you in no uncertain terms that they were Hudson Valley bluebloods.

At the other end of the spectrum is the French Louis XVI style parlor with its worn upholstery and tattered gold silk wall coverings that must make conservators feel uneasy. But there's something very poignant and realistic about the room. You can so easily picture Daisy sitting there as straight as her old bones would allow, the grand dame of a faded era, still proudly holding onto her century of memories. And what greater contrast could there be in this once-magnificent home then the tiny kitchen where Daisy sat alone in her final years at a small table with an old toaster, thinking back to the days when servants were at her beck and call?

Wilderstein is a very personal experience, and perhaps that is in part because something of the people who lived there still lingers in the now dark and empty halls that once bustled with activity. Daisy spoke of the spirit of a woman in the house with her, and like many of her generation, when younger she dabbled in Ouija boards and séances, which were then considered more of parlor games than any serious spiritualism.

However, she must have had some belief in the other world as in later years she always kept a newspaper clipping close to her that described the claim of an Irish medium who allegedly was in contact with the spirit of FDR and reported that he was having a "perfectly grand time."

Visitors to Wilderstein have also sensed the presence of spirits in the house, but they always describe them as being contented and only there because they loved the house and choose to remain. Staff members and volunteers also catch the distinct scent of a woman's perfume on the second floor, another gentle reminder that the house is not as empty as it appears.

There was one actual sighting—a visitor who said she was psychic claimed she saw a woman in a maid's outfit working at the kitchen sink. The woman's body was crooked and bent at odd angles. She indicated that she had been a servant and had fallen from a horse during a riding accident and died on the property, so perhaps out of a sense of duty she has returned to the chores she left unfinished?

Regardless of your beliefs, the recurring theme here is that people—and perhaps spirits—are working at Wilderstein today because they love it and want to preserve it for future generations to enjoy. Few will ever be able to call such a place home, but everyone can have the opportunity to take some time to visit the house, walk the grounds, and for a short time at least, feel as though they are part of Wilderstein's extended family.

Recommendation

Visit Wilderstein if you have any interest in Hudson Valley history, architecture, FDR, landscaping, decorative arts, or the story of a woman who lived to see almost the entire twentieth century.

Whereas some of the huge mansions along the Hudson can feel impersonal and somewhat intimidating, Wilderstein is a totally different experience. From the moment you enter the house to watch a brief film in which Daisy and her sister speak fondly about their home, you feel like a welcome guest. Although generations of people lived here and visited the place, ultimately it is Daisy who epitomizes the history of Wilderstein, and today Wilderstein is a living representation of Daisy. The house stands as a monument to the resilience of its former owner, and the dedication of many talented staff members and volunteers.

This is a site that deserves a slow and careful eye to appreciate the myriad of details inside and out, as well as a casual stroll along the garden paths where so many of the rich and famous spent their happy idle hours.

Visitor Information

Wilderstein
330 Morton Road
Rhinebeck, New York 12572
(845) 876-4818

Regular Tour Season:

May 1 to October 31, Thursday to Sunday, noon to 4 pm. House museum open for guided tours. Last tour is at 3:30 pm. Group tours also available by reservation.

There are special events such as art exhibits and high teas throughout the season. For updated information, go to: www.wilderstein.org/calendar.html.

There is a gift shop on the premises. The property is available for weddings and special events.

Wilderstein's grounds are open year-round from dawn until dusk and there is no charge to walk the grounds and trails.

Admission

Adults $10, students and seniors $9, children under 12 free.

Directions

As listed on their Web site:

From the Center of Rhinebeck: South on Route 9 to First Right (Mill Road).

Turn Right on Mill Road (next to cemetery) and take Mill Road 2.2 Miles to first right (Morton Road/County Route 85).

Make a right turn onto Morton Road and proceed 1/4 mile to Wilderstein Entrance on left.

From Hyde Park/Staatsburg: North on Route 9 which will widen to four lanes north of Staatsburg and narrow again to two lanes. Continue until the first possible left (Mill Road).

Turn left on Mill Road (next to cemetery). Follow Mill Road for 2.2 miles until the first right, which is Morton Road.

Make a right turn onto Morton Road and proceed 1/4 mile to Wilderstein Entrance on left.

The Bottom Line

The History: The home of a woman who had a close relationship with one of the most famous men in history, containing an amazing archive of 150 years of American life. Due to thousands of documents, photos, and letters, the story of a family through good times and bad is wonderfully preserved.

The Haunting: The scent of a woman's perfume, the crooked figure of a former servant, and the pervading sense that many contented spirits are throughout the house and grounds.

The Depuy Canal House, High Falls.

Depuy Canal House
Short History of the Delaware & Hudson Canal

As painful as gas prices are today, it would be hard to imagine what would happen if the flow of oil from the Middle East suddenly stopped. Such reliance on foreign energy is a precarious position to be in, and surprisingly it is nothing new. Almost 200 years ago, our young and growing country faced its own energy crisis. The British had been supplying coal for us to heat our homes and cook our food, but during the War of 1812, those shipments stopped and Americans quickly realized they needed domestic sources of coal.

There were vast deposits of coal in Pennsylvania, but no easy way to transport it to where it was needed. In a bold plan, the Wurts brothers undertook the building of a 108-mile canal from Honesdale, Pennsylvania, to Eddyville, New York, in the country's first million-dollar, privately-financed business venture. The gamble paid off, and by 1828, coal was flowing to the Hudson River on barges pulled by mules. The D&H Canal operated for seventy years until the railroad provided a faster and cheaper way to transport the coal.

The canal that was once the energy artery of America was abandoned and became overgrown, and many of the shops and businesses along the route that supported the canal and its workers were closed.

A Tavern Prospers

In 1797, Simeon Depuy had no idea that one day his new Stone House Tavern would prosper because Lock 16 of the D&H Canal would be built nearby. Canal men were hard working and hard drinking, and the tavern was the perfect place for good food and plenty of liquor to wash it down.

Those good times ended when the canal closed in the early 1900s, and the tavern was eventually left vacant. Local resident John Novi was interested in the history of the canal, and saw potential in the old stone building. In 1964 he purchased the property for $4,500 (the asking price had been $12,000) and began years of planning and restoration. Fortunately, John wanted to keep the original fireplaces, floorboards, and decorative woodwork, so the character and historical integrity of place was preserved.

The Herculean tasks complete, John's dreams finally came to fruition in 1969, when he opened the Simeon Depuy Tavern as a fine dining restaurant featuring his own American Nouvelle Cuisine. Remarkably, within only a year, the restaurant received a four-star rating from *New York Time's* food critic Craig Claiborne, and forty years later, John and the Depuy Canal House continue to earn glowing reviews.

Of course, along the way there have been some bumps in the road, as well as quite a few things that have gone bump in the night. One of the first odd things to happen occurred in the restaurant's early days. Back then, John was living in rooms upstairs and his partner, Kevin Zraly (Wine Director of Windows on the World from 1976 – 2001, and author of *Windows on the World Complete Wine Course*) was living downstairs. Every night they had a set routine of steps, like taking out the garbage, locking the door to the bar, locking the outside doors, etc.

One night after closing, Kevin knocked on John's door. John asked what was wrong, and with some urgency and concern in his voice Kevin replied that something was going on and he would have to come and see for himself. John went downstairs and found the previously locked bar door standing wide open and the water faucets were gushing full blast!

On many other occasions, John has seen flickering and flashing lights under closed doors, and heard strange sounds. One night, the lights were so bright and the sounds so clear he thought that the fireplace in the room must still have a crackling fire blazing. However, when he opened the door he was surprised to find that there wasn't any fire burning, no lamps were on, and there was absolutely nothing to explain the lights or the sounds he had heard. There weren't even any windows in the room, so the lights and noises could not have come from the outside.

Strange phenomena such as this have happened regularly throughout the Depuy Canal House over the past four decades, but John takes it all in stride. He believes there is some force that remains after we die, and the force in this case has always seemed to be supportive. Perhaps old Simeon has even lent a helping hand on several occasions. For example, one of the reasons the selling price was so low was that there were some questions about supplying water to the house which might prevent the restaurant from opening.

One day, John was just taking a stroll across the street and happened to come upon an artesian well. He traced the owner of the property, who sold him the land and its fresh, clean water supply for just $100. When digging for the pipes to bring the water to the house, workers informed John that they would have to jackhammer a hole through the three-foot-thick stone walls, which promised to be a costly and messy ordeal. However, when they reached the wall with the pipe, they found that at that exact spot, there already was just the right diameter hole!

"I immediately opened a bottle of champagne," John said recalling that happy coincidence. "Then we found out that a Father Divine had originally dug the well, so we always called it our Divine Water."

If Simeon or any of his family do still reside here in some manner, they definitely approve of how John has lovingly restored their home and revived the tradition of serving good food and spirits— although fortunately the average patron today is not quite like the canal workers of the past!

From the beginning, John Novi saw himself as simply the caretaker of this historic property. Hopefully, future generations will also preserve and protect its memories and traditions. They had better, because Simeon will be keeping an eye on them...

Recommendation

You could just drive by and admire the exterior, but why do that when there are so many delectable things to admire on the menus, while sitting in one of several beautiful dining areas. From a light lunch, to sushi, to an extravagant dinner with fine wines, you can absorb the history of this place by one of the fireplaces and truly have a wonderful taste of another time. Award-winning cuisine in an authentic two-centuries-old stone building, what's not to love? They even have accommodations at their Locktender Cottage right across the street.

Visitor Information

Depuy Canal House
Route 213, Box 96
High Falls, New York 12440
845-687-7700
office@depuycanalhouse.net
www.depuycanalhouse.net

There are three separate dining options:
Depuy Canal House Fine Dining Restaurant: Dinner Friday thru Sunday 5 pm to 10 pm.

Sunday brunch 9 am to 2 pm. Chefs on Fire Bistro: Wednesday 4:00 pm - 10 pm. Thursday - Sunday 11 am - 10 pm.

Breakfast on Saturday and Sunday Brunch 9am to 2pm.

The New York Store (Cafe): Open 7 days a week 7 am to 7 pm.

There are special events such as wine tastings, and they host weddings and parties. Call or check their Web site for the latest calendar of events, and for information on overnight accommodations.

Directions

From the South: Take the New York State Thruway to Exit 18 (New Paltz). Turn left, westbound on Route 299. Turn right onto Route 32 North in New Paltz and go 8 miles to Rosendale. Turn left onto Route 213 West. The Depuy Canal House is located approximately 3.5 miles on the left, across from the Locktender Cottage.

From the North: Take the New York State Thruway to Exit 19 (Kingston). Take the exit (Route 28 West) off the traffic circle to Route 209 South towards Ellenville. At the south end of Stone Ridge, turn left onto Route 213 East and go 1.5 miles to High Falls. The Depuy Canal House is on the right, across from the Locktender Cottage.

The Bottom Line

The History: A tavern opened in 1797 that became a popular spot throughout the 1800s with workers on the D&H Canal. Left vacant for years, it was purchased in 1964, and restored by award-winning chef John Novi. The Depuy Canal House is now making its own history with imaginative American cuisine.

The Haunting: Locked doors have opened, and there have been decades of many strange sounds and lights. There is a strong presence here, perhaps of Simeon Depuy himself?

What do the Brooklyn Bridge, Statue of Liberty, Washington Monument, and the U.S. Capitol have in common? They all used Rosendale cement in their construction. Today, we all take this common building material for granted, but good cement was a precious commodity in the early 1800s.

Thousands of workers came to Rosendale to dig limestone (used to make the cement) out of the surrounding hills. In addition to the many famous structures that contain Rosendale cement, it was used locally to build the D&H Canal. With the influx of all the canal workers and the miners, the once-quiet town became the scene of countless bars and brawls.

Obviously, with so much drinking going on, one thing was bound to happen—drunks would fall into the canal and drown. In fact, there were many people who drowned in the canal, both as the result of drinking, and simply by accident, taking a wrong step in the dark of night. There was one particularly

dangerous curve known as Dead Man's Stretch, between Main Street and Lawrenceville, where many unfortunate souls met their end. As a result, this area got the reputation for being haunted.

Rosendale

An old postcard depicting Dead Man's Stretch in Rosendale.
Courtesy of the Rosendale Library.

A postcard view of Main Street in Rosendale.
Courtesy of the Rosendale Library.

Spirits Lurk

Other spirits also lurk throughout the town, including:

The mysterious woman in black has been seen in many locations.

The "water witch," is said to rise out of the mists of the Rondout at night.

A girl was murdered at the Rock Lock, and her ghost was seen on an abandoned boat left to rot there.

One of the caves is supposed to have the spirits of an Indian boy and a farmer's daughter. The girl's uncle was trying to shoot the boy, and the couple fled into the cave. An accidental shot caused a cave-in, and the two were never seen again.

In the late 1800s, the canal closed, and the faster drying Portland cement killed the Rosendale cement industry. However in 2004, Rosendale cement was once again being manufactured as its high quality was rediscovered. Buildings undergoing restoration, such as the Museum of Natural History in New York City, are happy to be able to make repairs with the same color and texture cement they used over a hundred years ago.

Will new ghost stories arise as the cement industry is revived? Perhaps, but even if they don't, the town of Rosendale has enough spooky tales connected with the caves, streets, and the old canal to keep any ghost hunter busy.

Recommendation

Keep a sharp lookout for cave entrances in and around Rosendale. Walk the streets of town and imagine what the place would be like when all the miners and canal workers came to town on payday!

Directions

From the South: Take the New York State Thruway to Exit 18 (New Paltz). Turn left, westbound on Route 299. Turn right onto Route 32 North in New Paltz and go 8 miles to Rosendale.

From the North: Take the New York State Thruway to Exit 19 (Kingston). Take the exit (Route 28 West) off the traffic circle to Route 209 South towards Ellenville. At the south end of Stone Ridge, turn left onto Route 213 East to Rosendale.

The Bottom Line

The History: The town was an important center for cement production in the 1800s and the D&H Canal brought an influx of canal workers.

The Haunting: The canal and the caves are considered haunted. Various spirits have been witnessed throughout the streets of town.

The Shanley Hotel, Napanoch.

The Shanley Hotel is in the small town of Napanoch, which was once a bustling tourist area for the rich and famous. Visitors would arrive by train and spend their days in the surrounding woods and mountains, and then enjoy the cool evening breezes on the hotel's spacious front porch.

The first hotel on the site was the Hotel Napanoch built in 1845. It was a smaller structure, and it burned down in March of 1895. Just six months later, they were already plastering the walls of the new, larger hotel. While some of the wealthiest tourists stayed at the exclusive Yama Farms Inn nearby, the men would still come to the Hotel Napanoch at night as it had something their fancier counterpart did not—a bar!

Something of a *Who's Who* of celebrities and notable people passed through the doors of the hotel in the late nineteenth and early twentieth centuries, including Eleanor Roosevelt, but it was to also have a less reputable history. In 1905, James Shanley bought the hotel. His family owned several restaurants in New York City, and while the establishment continued to thrive under his experienced management, he also began some shadier enterprises.

In 1932, the Shanley Hotel was raided by federal marshals on two occasions, as Mr. Shanley was caught running a bootlegging operation (dealing in illegal liquor during Prohibition). Also, an addition was built to the back of the bar area in 1910, and this structure reputedly became a brothel. Of course, such a business would not be listed with the Better Business Bureau so there is no documented evidence that has yet come to light, but many local residents have confirmed that this oldest of professions was practiced at Shanley's until very late in the twentieth century.

Mr. Shanley died in the mid-1930s, and as none of his three children lived beyond six months, the hotel passed into the hands of other owners. The glory days were long gone in its final decades, and the place shut down in 1992. The old hotel remained vacant and crumbling until Sal and Cindy Nicosia purchased the property in 2005. They have beautifully restored and decorated the place, and the Shanley Hotel is once again open for business—although there are a few things you need to know before you book your reservations.

When asked about the paranormal experiences in the building, Sal and Cindy just laughed as if to say, "Where should we start?" And it was difficult to say what came first—the footsteps, voices, shadowy figures or the feelings of a strong presence. Because so much has occurred over the past several years, just some of the more dramatic highlights are presented below:

One night, soon after Sal and Cindy moved into their second floor rooms, they heard very loud footsteps coming up the staircase from the first floor. Their initial thoughts did not involve ghosts as the footsteps sounded so real. They thought that perhaps someone in town had seen lights on in the hotel, and not realizing the long-derelict structure was once again occupied had called the police. However, when they went to see if a cop was on their staircase, they found no one. Sal searched the rest of the house and found that all of the doors and windows were securely locked, and no other living person was in the building.

Much of the activity takes place in the former bar area. One night, they placed a baby monitor in the large room, then sat upstairs and listened. Very shortly afterward they heard voices and movement, as if the bar was back in operation. Again thinking it was living intruders, Sal came downstairs and unlocked the door to the bar. The moment he stepped inside the sounds abruptly stopped. However, as soon as he closed and locked the door again, the sounds of voices and activity began again. Cindy then came downstairs and told the spirits to "knock it off," and finally there was peace and quiet.

There's also the "balancing acts," as they call them. Their grandson tossed his toy penguin to the floor, and it landed on its head and stayed perfectly upright and motionless as if being held in place. As this toy penguin was just as bottom heavy as the living varieties, everyone was amazed to see this lopsided toy perfectly balanced upside down. Ever since then, they have tried to make the penguin stand on its head, with absolutely no success. They have also found other objects strangely balanced.

There are many cold spots, as well as the more rare hot spots. The smell of cigar smoke often hangs in the air, although no one smokes cigars. Clothes and hair have been tugged, there have been several incidents of being pushed (as if someone was trying to get by), radio dials spin, doors open, and there was the sound of a clock chiming the hour, when there were not yet any clocks in the building.

Mr. Shanley had a secret room under the coat closet where he used to conduct his bootlegging business. Many people have had to flee that room in a hurry as feelings of fear and panic sweep over them.

In the former brothel rooms women in particular feel disoriented and have trouble standing up straight because it feels as if the floor is moving, even though there's nothing wrong with the floor.

The staircase leading up to the third floor is one of the areas where people have seen the "Piano Man." Several decades ago, a poor, elderly man who lived in the hotel used to play the piano to earn a few tips in the bar. Despite being essentially destitute, he always dressed in a very dapper manner, and his ghost still appears well-dressed and groomed. He also continues to play the piano, as several people have heard music, although until recently, there wasn't even a piano in the place!

In the late 1980s, a regular patron of the bar went into the bathroom and came face-to-face with a stern looking woman in a Victorian-era dress. The man ran terrified from the bathroom and refused to ever step back in there. However, his fear didn't prevent him from returning to the bar on a regular basis. It was just that from that day, whenever nature called, he would go home to use his own bathroom, then return to the bar!

This is just the tip of the haunted iceberg. Things happen at all times of day on every floor and in every room. Much has transpired within the walls of this hotel, including several deaths, and it appears that the result of all of these events is that something of the past is still active here today. The Shanley Hotel has a long and colorful history, and as their motto says, at the Shanley "The Spirits are Inn."

Recommendation

This may be one of the most haunted places in the entire Hudson Valley. If you are brave enough, you can spend the night here, as it is now a bed and breakfast. They also have scheduled public ghost hunts, or you can arrange one for your own group. If you aren't quite that brave and still want to experience Shanley's firsthand, there are lectures and special events throughout the year. If you have any interest in haunted places (and you must, or you wouldn't be reading this now) you can't miss the opportunity to spend the night with a few ghosts!

Visitor Information

Shanley Hotel
56 Main Street
Napanoch, New York 12458
Cynthia Nicosia (Owner/Proprietor)
(845) 210-4267   cindy@shanleyhotel.com
Salvatore Nicosia (Owner/Proprietor)
(845) 467-7056   sal@shanleyhotel.com
Web site: www.shanleyhotel.com

Reservations are required for all guests for overnight stays and ghost hunts. Reservations are suggested for lectures and special events. Go to their Web site or call for rates and the latest calendar of events.

Directions

As listed in their Web site:

Take exit 19 (Route 28/Kingston/Rhinecliff Bridge) on the New York State Thruway. Then bear right onto RT-28 West. In .5 miles, take Exit 209 Ellenville. Stay on 209 South (24.8 mi). You will pass the township of Stone Ridge, Accord, Kerhonkson, before reaching Napanoch. Pass first light; on right you will approach the Napanoch Mall; next will be Peter's Market. Turn right at Peter's Market onto Main Street. Pass Hugenot Street; third building down on right (corner of Main and Clinton Street) is the Shanley Hotel.

The Bottom Line

The History: A popular hotel from 1845, with many famous guests over the years. Also the site of a bootlegging operation and brothel. Closed in 1992, but restored and reopened as a bed and breakfast in 2008.

The Haunting: Where to begin? Figures, voices, sights, smells, sounds, and sensations of all types. If you are serious about wanting to experience haunted activity in the Hudson Valley, attend one of Shanley's ghosts hunts or spend the night.

Legend has it that there is a real ghost town on Lundy Road in the town of Wawarsing. The story goes that it was built on land that the Indians considered haunted. Tragedies struck the town in the form of fire and floods. Then a prominent citizen killed his entire family and hung himself. The town was eventually abandoned, but spirits still linger and terrorize those brave, or foolish, enough to venture back into the deep, dark woods.

The actual history is that the town, called Pottersville, began in the 1850s when Francis Potter built a saw mill, and homes for the workers soon sprang up around it. The mill burned in 1870 and the Potters moved away, as did most of the workers and their families. Pottersville was occupied again early in the twentieth century, but a flood in 1928 caused the town to be abandoned for the second time. In the 1930s, Frederick Lundy purchased the town and eventually bought thousands of acres surrounding it.

Lundy was famous for his Lundy's seafood restaurant in Sheepshead Bay, Brooklyn, which claimed to be the largest restaurant in the country with seating for 2,800. Lundy was an eccentric recluse, which was possibly the result of a history of personal tragedies. Both of his parents and three of his brothers died before he was twenty-five. Two of his business associates were shot, and he was robbed and actually kidnapped on one occasion.

He did not want strangers near his property and women were never allowed in the mansion he built on Lundy Road. Guests slept in cabins or tents. In his last years, Lundy (who came to be called the Howard Hughes of New York) lived in rooms over his restaurant where his paranoia caused him to order that all of the windows be painted over so no one could see in. He died in 1977.

Lundy Road
The Vanishing Ghost Town

Today, the Lundy mansion is in new hands and is being restored. However, 5,400 acres of the land is now the property of New York State and will be protected open space. While this is a boon to conservationists, it signaled the death of the ghost town. In order to return the area to its natural state, all of the houses and buildings were bulldozed and burned.

However, while the buildings may be gone, does that mean the spirits have also moved on? Probably not, if one is to believe the many encounters and experiences people have had driving and hiking along Lundy Road. But before you take a look for yourself, there are two words of caution.

When you first turn onto Lundy Road, it seems like a typical street with a cluster of houses. That all changes very quickly. The road narrows, large trees grow right along the edge of the road, and suddenly there's a whole lot of nothing. If you have a keen eye, you may be able to pick out an old stone chimney or foundation wall here and there in the woods.

Eventually, you pass the old Lundy Mansion, then the road really gets hazardous. You are definitely in 4-wheel drive territory from this point, so parking and hiking may be the wiser choice once the road becomes too difficult. However, six or seven miles in from the highway, you will in due course reach the remains of Pottersville. But even if you don't get that far, strange things apparently happen the length of the road, so at any point you may experience something.

Which brings us to the other word of caution. Beware of the living, as well as the dead, and respect Mother Nature. Hunting accidents have led to at least one death here in recent years. (Actually, a man shot his friend, so perhaps it wasn't an accident.) The woods are thick and can be disorienting. Don't wander off alone, and make sure you have a flashlight as darkness falls quickly in these woods.

Other than that, you are on your own on Lundy's Road, or are you?

Recommendation

You can easily drive on Lundy Road for several miles, but to get all the way to Pottersville requires 4-wheel drive with good ground clearance, or a good hike. Ghost stories are associated with many of the former structures, but the woods themselves are reputedly haunted, as well. Just be careful, and if you plan on being there at night, make sure you have a flashlight.

Directions

Lundy Road is off of Route 209/55 in the town of Wawarsing, just north of Napanoch.

The Bottom Line

The History: An abandoned town that was begun in the 1850s. Destroyed by a fire, then a flood. Bulldozed and burned in recent years to return the land to its natural state.

The Haunting: Hundreds of years ago, the Indians considered the land to be haunted. Generations of stories abound about ghosts connected with the old town, as well as the surrounding woods.

Hurley

In our high-tech, throwaway society, something that is five years old may be considered ancient. So it could be difficult for the modern mind to wrap itself around the concept of a town being almost 350 years old. Today, being somewhere with poor cell phone service is thought to be a major hardship, but think about the early inhabitants of Hurley who had to struggle for the basic necessities, while living under the constant threat of Indian attacks.

Admittedly, it is something of a culture shock to exit the roar of the traffic on the New York State Thruway and within minutes be driving down a street filled with buildings older than the United States itself. It is truly another world here—a world filled with an amazing history of Indian raids, Revolutionary struggles, spies, hangings, buildings being burnt to the ground, slaves turned abolitionists, secret rooms, and generations of family histories still being written.

The settlement began in 1661 with twelve Dutch and Huguenot families from Kingston. In Nieuw Dorp (New Village) they built their wooden homes and hoped to lead quiet lives farming the fertile soil along the Esopus Creek. However, the Esopus Indians had other ideas. In 1663, angered by the way the Dutch treated them, the Indians attacked and burned the settlers' houses. Three men were killed, and thirty-five people were taken as hostages. It took a year to rescue all of the settlers, but peace was eventually restored and the rebuilding could begin.

Learning a valuable lesson from the Indian raid, this time they built their homes with stone. After the British seized control of New York from the Dutch, Nieuw Dorp was renamed Hurley, after the English ancestral home of the new governor. It was a peaceful transition, the village continued to grow, and the decades passed quietly—until the British became a problem.

The quiet little village was suddenly thrust into the spotlight in October of 1777 when the British burned Kingston, which was then the capital of the New York. Refugees fled into town and the British were not far behind, continuing to burn homes and barns

The Van Deusen House on Main Street became the temporary state Capitol in 1777.

along the way. It looked like Hurley would be destroyed for the second time, but just after the British torched the Schepmoes House (on Hurley Avenue) they were ordered to retreat back to Kingston and the rest of the town was spared.

The Van Deusen House on Main Street became the temporary state Capitol as members of the emergency governing body, the Committee of Safety, met in the parlor (or possibly the dining room, the exact location isn't certain). All of the important state documents were hidden in the house's secret room—a windowless room that could only be accessed from a trap door in the ceiling of a kitchen closet! It may not have been the most grand and elaborate of capitol buildings and document archives, but from November 18 to December 18, 1777, this unassuming stone house was the Capitol of New York State.

The Continental Army was also in town, with the soldiers encamped along Main Street. The Wynkoop Tavern became General Clinton's headquarters, and the Half Moon Tavern provided room and board for other officers and staff. Guards were posted along all the roads leading to town, and such a presence of patriot soldiers should have caused any British spies traveling in the area to turn and run, except

in one bizarre case. An unusual twist of fate led to one spy meeting his fate by twisting on the end of a rope.

A shipment of British uniforms heading for Burgoyne's army had been seized and brought to Boston Harbor. The uniforms made their way to Colonel Samuel Webb's Connecticut Regiment. Webb's men were standing guard in Little Britain, to the south of Hurley, when Lieutenant Daniel Taylor of the 9th Royal Regiment rode into town. He had been dispatched to deliver a message from General Henry Clinton at Fort Montgomery to Burgoyne's army north of Albany, and was wearing civilian clothing to escape detection.

Unfortunately for Lieutenant Taylor, when he saw all of the soldiers wearing the distinctive British red coats, he thought he was among friends and his true identity was revealed. If ever a man was in the wrong place at the wrong time! While he was technically only a messenger, not a spy, he was a British soldier on a secret mission dressed as a civilian in enemy territory, and that added up to being a spy who would be sentenced to death.

Taylor was brought to Hurley and held in the DuMond House. On October 18, 1777, this unlucky messenger was brought across the street to Schoolhouse Lane were he was hung from an apple tree. His body remained hanging in the tree for two days as all of the soldiers in the area were paraded by to send a not-so-subtle message to anyone who might be considering spying for the British.

While freedom from the British was ultimately achieved, not all residents of Hurley enjoyed the benefits of liberty. In 1797, a slave girl was born on the estate of Colonel Johannes Hardenbergh. She grew up speaking Dutch, and working in the Hardenbergh House on Schoolhouse Lane until she was sold when she was eleven-years-old. While her given name was Isabella Baumfree, after gaining her freedom she was to take the name of Sojourner Truth and went on to become a preacher and famous abolitionist. Throughout Sojourner's many travels and long life, she never forgot what it was like to be born a slave, and never lost the Dutch accent from her early years in Hurley.

With hundreds of years of dramatic human history having taken place within the walls of the stone homes of Hurley, it would appear to make this place a prime location for spirits to linger. In fact, there are many ghost stories connected with the original twenty-five stone homes, as well as in the neighboring "newer" homes built in the 1800s. However, as they are mostly still private residences, the home owners are reluctant to reveal their exact locations. Fortunately, the owners of the most famous building in town, the Van Deusen House (built in 1723), are willing to share their stories of the spirit, or spirits, with whom they share their home.

When Jonathan and Iris Oseas bought the famous former Capitol of New York in 1969, there was already an old tradition of a haunting. In 1906, Dr. George W. Nash owned the house and complained that a ghost kept opening his back door. To prevent this mischievous spirit from disturbing his peace of mind, he installed an additional heavy-duty latch on the door. The latch still exists today, but it doesn't seem to have put a damper on the spirit's activities.

The first sign that the new owners had that they may not be alone came soon after moving in. The place needed many repairs, and

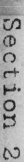

Jonathan—a level-headed scientist not prone to flights of fancy—was working on the plaster walls when he felt as if someone was watching him. No one was ever there, that he could see, but the strong sense of a presence remained, as if someone was overseeing his work to make sure everything was done properly.

An actual sighting did occur one night when their adult daughter awoke to see an Indian standing in her room. He was wearing what she described as "a Continental Army great coat," and he just stood there looking at her with great curiosity. She no doubt looked at him in the same way!

On another occasion, their daughter's boyfriend was spending the night in a different bedroom. Next to his bed on a night stand was an antique oil lamp with a shade, all made entirely of glass. Jonathan did not particularly care for this man, and the ghost of the Van Deusen house apparently shared his dislike. In the morning, the man awoke to find the lamp base, flue, and shade scattered across the floor, but not a single piece was broken. It was an effective way to scare the heck out of the man, without causing any damage.

For many years Iris and Jonathan have operated Van Deusen Antiques (originally inside the house, now in a shop at the end of the driveway) and dealers regularly came to do business. Several of them complained of hearing noises and footsteps in the house. Iris's response to one of the agitated dealers was, "I hear footsteps, too, but nobody is coming that you will see!"

Over the years, other visitors and guests have also reported feeling a presence and hearing sounds, and witnessing doors and cabinets opening on their own, but it has never been anything threatening. Iris believes that the spirits are simply curious and just want to keep an eye on the home in which they resided in life. The Van Deusen House is an historic treasure, and its friendly spirits are just more pieces its legacy.

Without divulging the names of the other houses, here's some of the other haunted activity in Hurley:

Mama!

One homeowner hears a young girl repeatedly calling for "Mama." The voice is only heard on the first floor, which is the oldest section of the house. Both the homeowner and her daughter have heard the girl call out, and it has happened several times a year for many years. Rather than be frightened, the owner decided to speak reassuring words to the girl, which has the effect of quieting the spirit!

Arrowhead Mischief

In this same house, a tenant had a collection of arrowheads he found while working on a local farm. The arrowheads, most likely from the Esopus Indians, were kept in a heavy case on a table. One day after returning from the farm, he found that the arrowhead case was on the floor. It hadn't fallen off the table, as nothing was damaged and all the arrowheads were in place. The case had obviously been lifted and placed on the floor. As he lived alone and had the only key, it was quite a mystery. The next day, he came home to find the case on the floor once again. He felt there must be the spirit of a local Indian causing the mischief, and quickly removed the arrowheads from the house.

A Fall

In a house where the same family had lived for over 150 years, the last living descendant was an elderly spinster. She was alone in the house, and in an unfortunate accident, fell to her death down the cellar stairs. It was three days before her body was discovered. From that day, the basement door would not stay closed, often swinging open on its own.

Opinions Have Their Place

Another home has a ghost that makes her presence known so frequently she has been given a name, the name of a former owner who died in the house. This spirit just doesn't seem to realize she's dead and walks about the house opening and closing doors at all times of the day and night. Her heavy breathing can also be heard and felt—an icy cold breath that may suddenly pass across your face. She isn't threatening in the least, but has been described as being "a bit clumsy and opinionated," which is no doubt a reflection of traits she had in life.

A Clanging Ghost

For generations people claimed to see a spirit walking along on Hurley Avenue. He was apparently a noisy ghost, as witnesses heard chains clanking as he moved.

Recommendation

This place is definitely a step back in time. Check the map in front of the museum or pick up a printed map with descriptions of the twenty-seven homes, the church, and the old burial ground (the oldest visible inscription is from 1715). It's an easy drive, but it makes for a wonderful walk on a warm summer's day or a crisp autumn afternoon during foliage season. Of course, the best way to experience the place is to go inside the homes on Stone House Day in July (see info below).

Visitor Information

Hurley Heritage Society Museum
52 Main Street, Hurley, New York 12443
(845) 338-1661
http://hurleyheritagesociety.org

Open May-October, Saturday 10 am to 4 pm, Sunday 1 to 4 pm
There is a sign in front of the museum with a map of 27 historic places to see in town. Printed maps are available in the museum.

Van Deusen Antiques
59 Main Street, Hurley, New York 12443
Call (845) 331-8852 for antique shop hours.

Special Events

There are guided walking tours the last Sunday of each month throughout the season. There is a fee of $3 for adults, children under 12 are free.

Stone House Day is held annually on the second Saturday of July. On this day, several houses are open to the public and tours are given by guides in period attire. Admission is $2 for children 5–12 (children under 5 are free), $12 for students and seniors, and $15 for adults. Tickets are available at the church and near the stone houses on the day of the event. No reservations are needed.

The region is known for its sweet corn, and on the third weekend in August, the annual Hurley Corn Festival is held, with many different activities and food (including all kinds of food made from corn, of course). Admission is $3 for adults, children under 12 are free.

Directions

From New York State Thruway Exit 19: Bear right for Route 28 West. Proceed 0.5 miles and turn right on ramp for Route 209 South. Go south on US-209 for 2.3 miles. Turn right immediately after underpass (Wynkoop Lane) CR-29A. Proceed 0.2 miles and take the first right (old route 209) to Main Street, Hurley.

The Bottom Line:

The History: First settled in 1661, there are 350 years of history here, including an Indian raid, a Revolutionary War encampment, a spy, a hanging, buildings being burnt to the ground, a slave turned famous abolitionist, and a secret room that held state documents. The Van Deusen house was the capitol of New York during 1777. There are an amazing amount of places to see here in just this one small area.

The Haunting: A former owner of the Van Deusen House actually installed a special lock to try to keep the ghosts from coming in and out. There are footsteps throughout the house, objects have been moved, and a figure of an Indian was seen. The entire town has numerous accounts of ghosts in the old stone homes.

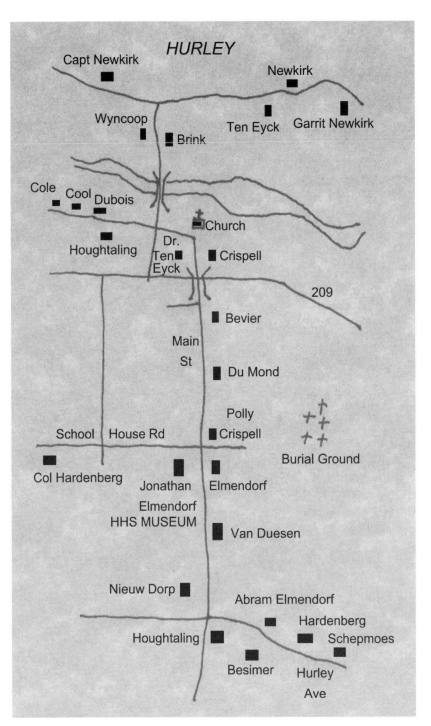

The historic sites in Hurley.

Declaring independence in 1776 was a bold and magnificent achievement in our nation's history. It was only the first step, however, as there was the business of winning a war and forming a new government. New York took its first steps into its new democracy in Kingston. There were no fine capitol buildings constructed for the twenty-four state senators—there wasn't exactly time for that with the British army breathing down their necks. No, there were far more humble beginnings in a rented room in the home of Abraham van Gaasbeek.

The house was originally built in 1676 by Colonel Wessel Ten Broeck, and if that seems ancient, consider the fact that the Dutch had already been living in Kingston for almost twenty-five years. In 1652, about seventy families had moved south from Albany to farm the fertile lands around the Esopus Creek. Dutch Governor Peter Stuyvesant recognized the importance of having a fort between Albany and New York City, and decided that a stockade should be built so the settlers—and the colony's commerce and trading interests—would be protected from the Indians. He named that settlement Wiltwyck.

Senate House

The Senate House in Kingston was New York's
first state Capitol.

The stockade was constructed in 1658 of upright logs, fourteen feet high, encompassing an area 1200 x 1300 feet, and containing forty houses. The settlers lived within the safety of its walls until 1664, when a peace treaty with the Indians was signed. However, the original layout of the streets of Wiltwyck still exists today, and the stockade stood for many years, with remnants of the 300-year-old timber fortifications still visible during an archaeological dig in 1971. (The dig took place on Clinton Street, near the Senate House.)

So, when the fledging New York State government needed a place to meet, it chose a house in a town that already had over a century of history. And while Abraham van Gaasbeek may have been a patriot, he was also a businessman. He had been operating a store in his house, but when the war interrupted his ability to restock with supplies from New York City, he saw an opportunity for some income by renting a room to the senators.

Despite any financial motivations, it was a very risky business, as van Gaasbeek and every senator was committing treason in the eyes of the British and could have lost their property and their lives. Fortunately, these men had the courage to take that leap of faith that America would ultimately prevail, so the old Dutch house became the cradle of New York government—its first State Capitol, today known as the Senate House.

Conditions for forming a government were certainly not ideal in the fall of 1777. In fact, the senators were only at work for four weeks at the van Gaasbeek house before they had to flee from the British. On October 6, Forts Montgomery and Clinton had been captured, leaving the door to Kingston (i.e., the Hudson River) wide open for the British. Fortunately, the senators and residents had enough advanced warning that they were able to flee, but the vacated town was put to the torch on October 16.

For the British, the burning of Kingston would amount to nothing more than a spiteful act of retribution, as Burgoyne would surrender at Saratoga the following day, making it pointless, and dangerous, to proceed any farther upriver. The British retreated and the residents of Kingston rebuilt their homes and businesses with a renewed patriotic fire. The senators were to go on to occupy a series of other meeting places, never returning to Kingston. But the Senate House was the first seat of government, and no matter where state politics takes us in the future, we can always point to the spot where it all began.

After the war, the house remained as a simple family home until it was acquired by New York State in 1887. An appeal was made to the community for historic items to display, and the outpouring was so great that a separate museum was built in 1927, directly behind the Senate House. Today, both the house and museum provide wonderful insight into the lives of the early Dutch settlers, the Revolutionary War period and the beginning of New York government, and the history of Kingston. There is also the largest collection of works by Kingston artist John Vanderlyn. (His *Landing of Columbus* is in the Rotunda of the Capitol in Washington, D.C., and his panoramic view of Versailles is in the American Wing of the Metropolitan Museum of Art.)

Romeo and Juliet—Wiltwyck Style

With so much history concentrated in a single location, does anything else from the past linger here? There is a charming old legend that suggests the spirits of two star-crossed lovers still meet here, seeking the joy they were denied in life. It is something of a Romeo and Juliet story, Wiltwyck-style.

The tale begins long ago, when a wealthy Dutchman lived in the house with his beautiful daughter. The man tried to keep his daughter isolated from the world in order to protect her, but one fateful night, a handsome Englishman came to the door. Despite the language barrier, it became apparent that the man was traveling from New York to Albany and needed a place to spend the night. Initially suspicious of the stranger, he appeared to be a man of wealth and refinement, so the Dutchman reluctantly admitted him into his home.

As words were useless, further attempts at conversation ended, but the Englishman saw another way to communicate. An old violin hung above the mantle, and he took it down and began to play the most beautiful music the Dutchman had ever heard. The daughter was also captivated, and emerged from the shadows to watch the Englishman play. The Dutchman was lulled to sleep by the soothing tones of the instrument, but when he awoke he found his daughter in the arms of the Englishman. The girl was sent to her room, and in the morning the unwelcome visitor was sent packing.

Undeterred by her angry father, the girl slipped away from the house each day to meet her love. After several days, the father discovered what was going on and locked his daughter in her room. The heartbroken Englishman waited and waited, but realizing it was hopeless, finally traveled on. The girl then sank into deep despair, and having lost her love, lost her will to live.

Seeing how gravely ill the girl had become and realizing how foolish he had been, the old Dutchman begged her forgiveness, but after two agonizing weeks, his daughter passed away. Her last request was that the violin be sealed inside the chimney of the fireplace where she and her lover first met. Legend has it that the handsome Englishman and the beautiful girl still meet by that fireplace, and when they do, those who know true love can hear the violin playing.

Recommendation

Regardless of how you feel about our current state government, remember the courage and sacrifice that it took to put New York on the road to democracy. In a rented room in this house, men gathered to lay the foundations of a system that still exists today. As you stand in that meeting room, think of what was happening at the time: The British were sailing up the Hudson and Burgoyne's army was coming from the north—not too much pressure on the senators!

On a domestic note, imagine preparing meals in the small, dimly-lit kitchen, which is actually twice its original size. And for those of a culinary bent, check out the 1820 sausage maker in the museum.

The museum has some wonderful items relating to Kingston, such as the Rent Wars mask, as well as a fine collection of furniture and artwork. The Vanderlyn paintings and sketches deserve a long look, and the knowledgeable staff can tell you all about his life and work. An absolute "must see" is the eye painting—perhaps the smallest portrait ever painted. Vanerdlyn had a mentor, none other than Aaron Burr, and he may have been smitten with Burr's daughter, Theodosia. He painted just her eye on a tiny circle of ivory, so be sure to look for it.

Also allow time to walk the old Dutch streets of the stockade district which still contains many historic buildings.

Visitor Information

Senate House
296 Fair Street
Kingston, New York 12401
Phone: (845) 338-2786
http://nysparks.state.ny.us.sites/info.asp?siteID=28

April 15 thru October 31 Monday, Wednesday, Saturday, 10 am to 5 pm, Sunday, 11 to 5 pm. Also open Memorial Day, Independence Day, and Labor Day. Site is open year-round by appointment.

Admission

$4 adults, $3 NYS senior citizens/groups. Children under 12 admitted free. Group tours year-round, must be scheduled in advance.

Directions

As listed in their Web site:
From Thruway (exit 19) traffic circle take Washington Avenue. At 2nd light, turn left onto Schwenk Drive, go 0.3 miles to Senate House. (A free parking lot is conveniently located across the street, directly in front of the Senate House.)

Bottom Line

The History: A house built in 1676 that became the site of the first state capitol when senators met here in 1777. Today, the Senate House is interpreted as it most likely appeared in 1777, with the early Dutch influences still evident. There is also a separate museum containing early American art, furniture, and items of local interest.

The Haunting: There is an old legend that the spirits of a pair of star-crossed lovers still meet by the fireplace, and when they do, violin music can be heard.

From just about anywhere in the old section of Kingston you can see a beautiful, tall, white spire. Since 1852, it has not only pointed the faithful toward heaven, it has acted in a more down to earth manner as a landmark by which to navigate the streets. Countless people see it every day, but few realize it has a strange legend attached to it.

The site once contained a stone church built in 1681 by a Dutch congregation that had formed in 1659. During the burning of Kingston in 1777, the British also destroyed the church, as the Dominie (pastor) was a staunch patriot. The present structure was built in the Renaissance Revival style, from the design of the influential American architect Minard Lafever. (Four of his buildings have been designated National Historic Landmarks.)

The cemetery's oldest burial record is from 1679, but it is likely there were earlier burials from the settlers in the 1650s. The oldest legible stone dates from 1710. Among the notable graves are those of seventy-one Revolutionary War veterans, and Governor and Vice-President George Clinton. There is also a graceful statue of a woman entitled "Patriotism," which was dedicated to the Civil War soldiers of the 120th New York Regiment by General George S. Sharpe. Both Sharpe and many members of the 120th were parishioners of the church.

There is so much history and the architecture to admire at ground level, yet one's eyes are inevitably drawn upward, and it is up this steeple where the legend begins. One day, an odd hat was seen perched on the very top of the steeple. The story spread that it was the cap of a goblin that resided within the spire. (We don't hear much about goblins today, but they were an important part of old Dutch folklore in the Hudson Valley.)

When the time came to have the steeple painted, only one man could be found who was brave enough to ascend the heights to the goblin's lair. The work proceeded without incident until the painter was near one of the small windows. There, he was suddenly stricken by an unknown illness. He was helped down to the ground, but quickly passed away.

The believers of the legend said that the man had died of fear because the goblin had made faces at him through the window. Then the tale turned ghostly when residents began to report seeing the figure of the painter high upon the steeple on stormy nights. This old legend took on a modern twist when, in recent times, another painter was hired. He supposedly quit because he kept feeling someone touching him when he was high up near that same window.

The tall steeple of the Old Dutch
Church in Kingston.

The Steeple

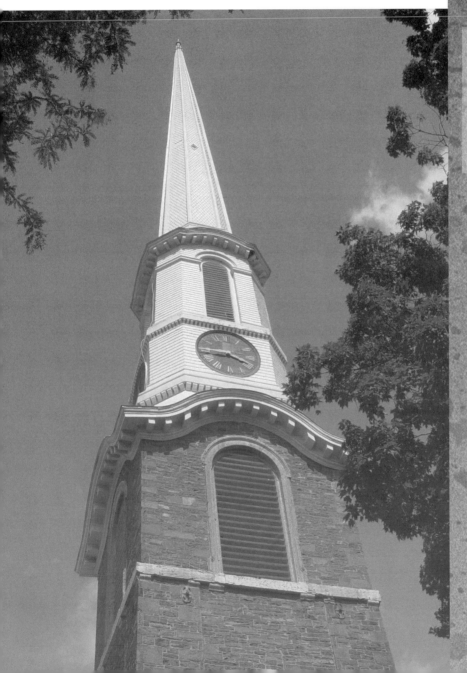

Is this steeple inhabited by a creature from folklore, and haunted by the unfortunate painter? The next time a storm is brewing over Kingston and lightning begins to flash, look up and see for yourself...

Visitor Information

The Old Dutch Church is located at the corner of Wall and Main Streets in Kingston. It is still an active church so please respect their privacy. The cemetery grounds are open to the public.

Directions

From the Thruway (exit 19) traffic circle take Washington Avenue. Turn left on North Front Street, then the third right on Wall Street. The church is two blocks down on your left.

The Bottom Line

The History: The site of a church first built in 1681 with a historic cemetery. The current church and its beautiful spire were constructed in 1852.

The Haunting: The spirit of a man who died painting the spire has been witnessed on stormy nights. Another painter felt someone touching him.

Huguenot Street

If a town is fortunate to have one historic structure, then New Paltz has an embarrassment of riches, and all on a single street.

Huguenot Street is one of the oldest continually inhabited streets in America, and it contains seven original stone houses, many of which were first constructed in the early 1700s. There is also a burial ground where many of early inhabitants are resting in peace—or not, if you believe the many accounts of restless spirits. But first the history:

Like many Europeans fleeing intolerance and persecution, the Huguenots came to this country to start a new life. Thanks to a land grant of 39,000 acres in 1678, twelve Huguenot families soon began creating their community of wooden houses, which later became the solid foundations of stone homes that still can be seen today. Over the generations the houses were expanded upon and updated, but in most cases, this was done without completely losing the character of the original structure. More than three centuries after the first houses were built here, Historic Huguenot Street still stands as a remarkable record of some of the first Europeans to call this section of the Hudson Valley home.

The Freer-Low House.

The Abraham Hasbrouck House.

Freer-Low House

Hugo Freer was one of the original Patentees of the land grant and family legend states that he escaped Europe hidden in a barrel. The house that we see today was most likely built by his son, Hugo, who began construction in the 1720s, with later additions. A descendant of Hugo Freer bought the house in 1943, and transformed the interior from its early Dutch design into a comfortable 20th century colonial revival style. In 1955, the home was purchased by the Huguenot Historical Society.

Abraham Hasbrouck House

Abraham Hasbrouck, also a New Paltz Patentee, arrived in America in 1675. In 1676, he married Maria Deyo, the daughter of another Patentee. (Abraham's brother, Jean, married Maria's sister, Anna.) Recent studies, including dendrochronology (tree ring dating taken from house beams), indicate that what we call the Abraham Hasbrouck House today, was actually built by Abraham's son Daniel starting around 1721, with two more additions added by 1741.

Bevier-Elting House

Precise dating for this stone house may never be entirely known, but it is generally accepted that Louis Bevier began building his house sometime in the early 1700s. Bevier was considered one of the wealthiest of the Patentees. His son, Samuel, made additions to the house in the 1720s and 30s to accommodate an ever-increasing household (nine children lived to maturity). Sometime in the mid eighteenth century, Samuel rented out one room of the house to Josiah Elting, an enterprising merchant. By the 1760s, the entire house had been purchased by the Elting family who maintained ownership of the building until 1963, when it was given to the Huguenot Historical Society.

Daniel DuBois House—The Old Fort

The DuBois family in New Paltz descended from wealthy linen merchants in Wicres, France. Louis DuBois and his wife emigrated to America in the early 1660s and settled in Niew Dorp (present day Hurley, New York). During the Esopus Indian Raid of 1663, Louis' wife and three of their children were taken hostage, but later released. His sons were original Patentees, inter-marrying with other members of the first twelve families. Louis' grandson, Daniel, built his family home in 1705 with features such as gun ports to comply, it is thought, with part of the original land grant that called for a fort or "redoubt." The house, which was greatly enlarged in the 1830s, was in the Dubois family until 1968 when it was purchased for the Huguenot Historical Society.

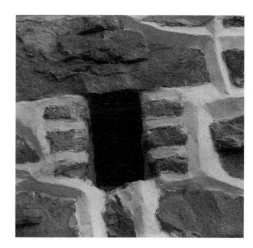

One of the Dubois house gun ports.

The Bevier-Elting House.

The Dubois House-The Old Fort.

Deyo House

Christian Deyo was born in France around 1610, and was the oldest of the twelve Patentees, dying in 1687 before the stone houses were built. Deyo House was probably built early in the eighteenth century by Christian's son, Pierre. The house remained in the Deyo family, but was extensively "modernized" in 1894 by a descendant (and one-time mayor of New Paltz), Abraham Deyo Brodhead. Although the original early eighteenth-century house has been altered with wood frame additions, portions of the old house are still visible both on the exterior and interior. The Brodheads moved out of the house in 1915. Two families lived there afterwards, until it was sold to the Huguenot Historical Society in 1971.

The Deyo House.

Jean Hasbrouck House

It has been concluded from recent investigations of the Jean Hasbrouck House (primarily using dendrochronology) that the construction date for this building is 1721. Jean Hasbrouck died in 1714, but it is likely that his son, Jacob, recycled some older materials from his father's home to build his house—the house that we see today. Jacob ran a general store from his residence (as did his son, Jacob, in the next generation). The configuration of the building is different from other houses on the street, with a long central hall and a very steep roof over storage space in the huge garret below. Hasbrouck's descendants lived in the house until it was purchased by the historical society—called at that time the Huguenot Monumental, Historical, and Patriotic Society—for use as their headquarters and the first museum house open to the public in 1899.

The Jean Hasbrouck House.

Elting House

Ezekiel Elting built his stone and brick house in 1799 in the elegant Georgian style which was very trend-setting for New Paltz at that time. Upon close inspection, one can see that he apparently had a limited amount of bricks at his disposal; these were used only for the front of the house and the top of the south elevation—the lower section of the south wall was stucco over stone, scored and painted to look like brick. The other two walls were left in the more traditional stone. Ezekiel ran a store on the first floor of his house. Sometime in the 1870s, the original Dutch gambrel roof was replaced with the current steeper-pitched roof, but the old roof line can still be seen in the attic.

The Walloon Church and the old burial ground.

Walloon Church and Burial Ground

The church is a 1972 reconstruction of the original. The burial ground contains many members of Huguenot Street's first families.

Haunted?

There is no doubt about this street being one the most historic streets in America, but is it also one of the most haunted? According to many eyewitness accounts, that answer may be yes. Every one of the sites has ghost stories connected with it, and here are just some of the highlights:

At the **Abraham Hasbrouck House**, the specter of a man in colonial-style clothing has been seen on the property. Witnesses say that the man is carrying an ax and is always followed by his ever-faithful ghostly black dog. They appear as if they are returning from some chore, and they both enter the house. Whether they enter through the door, or actually *through* the door isn't clear, but it is clear that neither of them is an earthly human or dog. Other reports claim that the man with the ax has been seen through an upstairs window, where he is yelling and raising the ax, as if about to strike.

Nearby in the **DuBois House**, there is the spirit of a woman, or at least, part of her. The woman wears a brown dress and walks the house in the dead of night. There are no other descriptions as to her appearance, due to the simple fact that she seems to be missing her head.

At the **Jean Hasbrouck House**, a spirit has been identified as that of Elizabeth Hasbrouck, who lived in the house until her death in 1928. Some people have claimed to have made direct contact with her ghost during a séance conducted there. The house also contains spinning wheels that mysteriously spin on their own.

In the **Deyo House** there are reports of a haunted painting, and portrait photographs that fly across the room.

There have been sightings of the ghost of a Hessian soldier at the **Bevier-Elting House**.

Recommendation

This is a perfect historical tour destination with so many fascinating places in such close proximity to one another. While you can drive by any time, it's well worth visiting in season to take a tour of the houses and hear about their history. A ghost tour is conducted during Halloween season if you want more details on the hauntings. After you learn the stories of these original families, take a stroll through the burial ground and see how many names you recognize.

Visitor Information

Historic Huguenot Street
18 Broadhead Avenue
(Between North Chestnut and Huguenot Streets)
New Paltz, New York 12561-1403
845-255-1660 Main Office
845-255-1889 Visitor Center (May through October only)

Guided tours are offered on a walk-in basis May through October, every day except Wednesday. The Tour Office and the DuBois Fort Visitor Center are open 10 am to 5 pm. Tours start on the hour. The last tour starts at 4 pm. Group tours are also available. Special events are held throughout the season, including ghost tours in October. For a full calendar of events, go to: http://www.huguenotstreet.org/about_us/calendar.html.

Admission

The standard tour is $7 for adults, $6 seniors, students, and Triple A members, $3 children 6-17, under 6 free, and includes an orientation and two houses.

The deluxe tour is $10 for adults, $9 seniors, students, and Triple A members, $5 children 6-17, under 6 free, and includes an orientation, three houses, and the church.

Directions

As listed on their Web site: http://www.huguenotstreet.org/about_us/directions.html

From the New York State Thruway: New York State Thruway (I-87) north to Exit 18, make a left onto Route 299. Travel west on Route 299, at the fourth traffic light make a right onto Rt. 32 North. Follow Rt. 32 through the next traffic light, go one block and make a left onto Broadhead Avenue. The HHS parking lot is just a few yards up on the left. You can walk from the parking lot to the Historic District & Visitor's Center.

The Bottom Line

The History: How could you not be interested in seeing one of America's oldest streets with houses dating to the early 1700s? Here, you will find documented histories of the original families who fled religious persecution to start a new life in the "wilderness" of New Paltz. There are many homes to explore, and an old cemetery where some of New Paltz's earliest settlers are buried.

The Haunting: There are too many stories to list all of them here, as all of the sites have ghostly activity. Some prime examples: there is a man carrying an ax, accompanied by his dog, there is a headless woman, and objects that move on their own.

Section Three

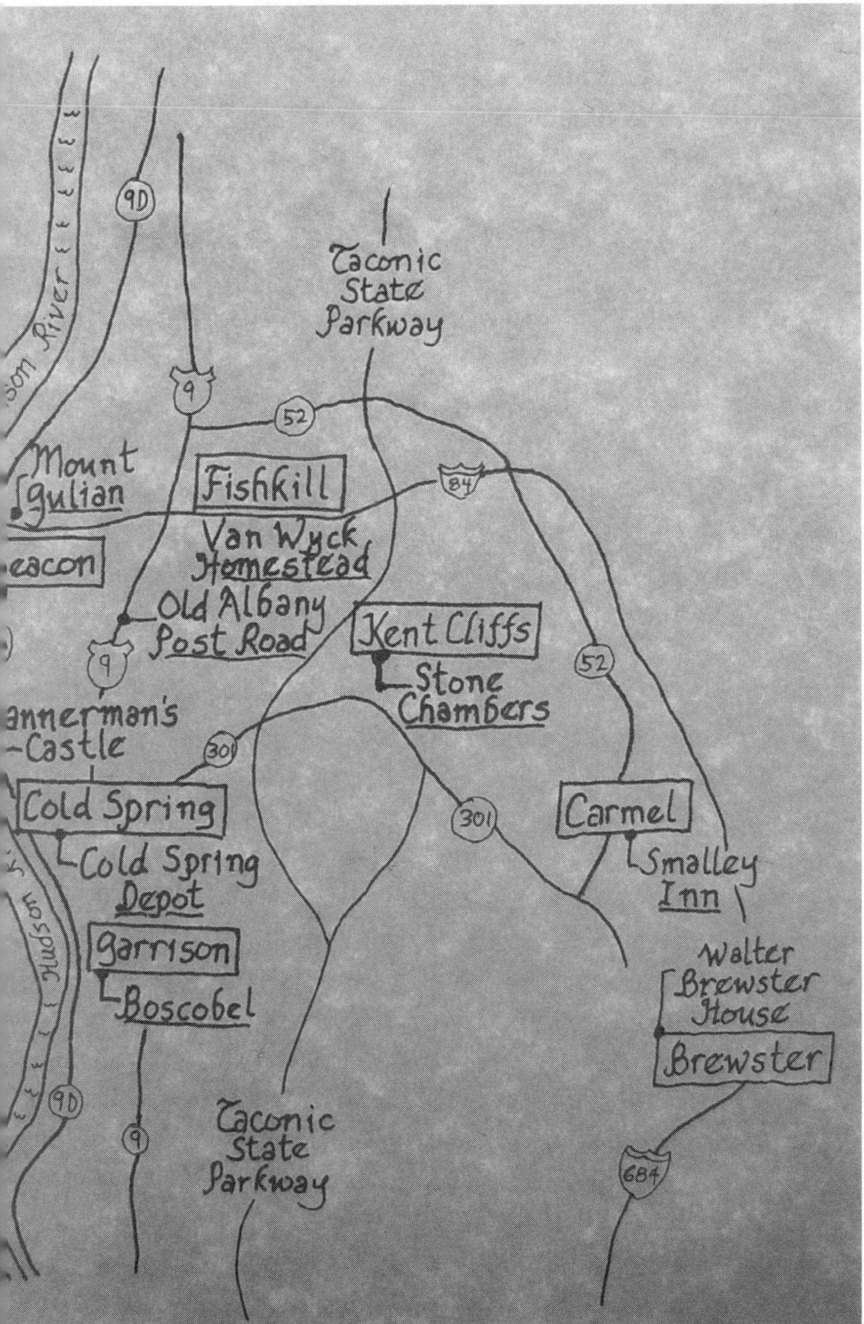

Mount Gulian Historic Site in Fishkill.

Mount Gulian

Driving through a typical suburban garden apartment complex, one would not expect to find anything of historical significance. However, in the town of Beacon there is a hidden treasure at the end of just such a development—Mount Gulian Historic Site, the former home of one of New York's oldest families, the Verplancks.

Of course, before any Europeans settled in the Hudson Valley, Native Americans called the banks of the river home for thousands of years. In fact, on this property, archaeological evidence indicates that they had been camping here as far back as 6,000 BC. After such a long period of habitation, it is remarkable to think how quickly they lost their ancestral lands.

Case in point: In 1683, the Wappinger Indians felt the relentless pressure of the European settlers and reluctantly sold 85,000 acres of land to Francis Rombout, Stephanus Van Cortlandt, and Gulian Verplanck. Known as the Rombout Patent, the land purchase cost the men a mere $1,200 worth of wampum, guns, clothing, tobacco, rum, and beer. One of the remarkable items in the Mount Gulian collection is the actual ceremonial pipe the Wappingers presented to Gulian Verplanck at the signing of the deed.

Verplanck made good use of this prime riverside land and increased the family fortune. While the Verplancks had a fine home in Manhattan, around 1730 they decided to build a house on the property. At first, it was just a summer home and a base of operations for their large plantation, the shipping dock in the river, and other business interests, and it wouldn't be for over seventy years until any Verplancks took up permanent residence in the house.

However, during that period, the Verplancks had some very interesting guests, such as Baron Von Steuben and the Continental Army. Samuel Verplanck was a prominent patriot and opened the house to the colorful Prussian general to use as a headquarters, which was an ideal location as it was close to other officer's headquarters and military barracks in the region.

Once victory was assured, Von Steuben, along with Henry Knox and other officers, formed the country's first fraternal organization, The Society of the Cincinnati, for officers who fought in the Revolutionary War, and their male descendants. At first the organization was viewed with suspicion, as Americans feared that these officers were attempting to form a new aristocracy, but 225 years later, the Society is the oldest and one of the most respected organizations of its kind—and it all began at Mount Gulian, which is still the Society's New York chapter headquarters.

In that unique brand of American hypocrisy, it must be pointed out that the patriotic, freedom-loving Verplancks, like many of our founding fathers, did own slaves who worked and lived on the property. However, over the years, their sentiments turned toward abolition, as is evidenced by James Brown, an escaped slave. While working as a waiter for the Verplancks, Brown was recognized, and would have been returned to slavery had the family not arranged for his freedom. Mary Anna Verplanck taught Brown to read and write, skills he put to good use by keeping a journal for the next forty years. Brown's story is a remarkable one, and his journals are a rare piece of African-American history.

In 1804, Daniel Crommelin Verplanck, a member of Congress, was the first to make Mount Gulian his permanent home. He built a large addition on the north side of the house—a rectangular frame structure totally out of character with the Dutch stone house—and added formal gardens, as well as numerous other buildings. His daughter, Mary Anna, proved herself to be a capable mistress of the house and plantation.

Another notable family member was Robert Newlin Verplanck, who was born in 1842. A Harvard graduate with all of the privileges money could buy, Robert nonetheless felt the call to duty during the Civil War, and in a special way—he was an officer in the United States Colored Troops. His eloquent letters written during the war provide a valuable record and fascinating insight into many of the important issues of the times.

The post-war years saw the Verplancks continue to prosper as they rubbed their sophisticated Victorian-era elbows with many of New York's elite families, such as the Livingstons, Roosevelts, and Vanderbilts. As the twentieth century dawned, Verplancks continued to achieve success and prominence in many different professions. The history surrounding the Verplancks and their 200-year-old home should have made Mount Gulian one the premier historic houses in all of America. Then tragedy struck.

On September 5, 1931, someone deliberately set fire to the house. Firefighters, police, and neighbors rushed to the scene and risked their lives to remove precious family heirlooms, Chippendale-style furniture, and priceless paintings. The wooden, early nineteenth-century addition was reduced to ashes, while all that remained of the 1730 stone house were the stones.

Suspicion immediately fell on "an eccentric one-eyed Negro" known as Deefy. Several structures in the area had recently burned and police knew there was an arsonist in their midst. However, to their credit, they released Deefy for lack of evidence—which didn't always prevent convictions where prejudice was involved. Further investigation revealed that it was actually a white man who had set the fires. Found to be mentally unstable, he was committed, but he was eventually released and went on to a long career with the Mass Transit Authority. Many years later he still freely spoke about burning down Mount Gulian.

Devastated by their loss, the family never envisioned the house being rebuilt, so they donated the rescued furniture, porcelain, and paintings to the Metropolitan Museum of Art in Manhattan, which created a Verplanck Room in the American Wing. Of particular note are several Verplanck portraits by the premier painter of the time, John Singleton Copley. With these treasures safe and secure, it appeared as though this would be the only visible legacy of the family.

However, a concerted effort by Verplanck descendants, members of the Society of the Cincinnati, and dedicated historians brought about a rise from the ashes. Using lumber from trees on the property, the original stone house was reconstructed in time for Bicentennial celebrations in 1976. Many family items have been donated to the collection and centuries worth of history have been brought to life once again.

While this place has been wonderfully restored, is there any evidence that anything else ever returned to the world of the living here? Remarkably, yes, and it was on that fateful day in 1931 as flames consumed the family home. Newspaper accounts record this incredible sighting:

Colonial Pair "Appears" in Steuben House Blaze
Beacon, N.Y., Sept. 26 (UP)

Reports of an apparition in the 200-year-old Verplanck homestead while flames destroyed the structure recently are being discussed here. Three persons said that while gazing at the burning building they saw outlined in the ruins the figure of an old Colonial gentleman with powdered wig, seated at a desk, writing. Near by stood a Colonial dame, holding a candle.

In fact, there were many credible witnesses, including police officers. Other descriptions say that the colonial man seemed very rushed and anxious to complete whatever he was writing, while the woman continued to move the candle closer to him as the light dimmed. As if the sighting itself wasn't astonishing enough, this was not a mere fleeting glimpse—the colonial couple was visible for a full thirty minutes! Their images vanished only when flames collapsed the floor of the second story.

While there have been no sightings of the mysterious colonial couple since the fire, there have been reports of feeling a presence. A former executive director of the site lived in an upstairs apartment. One night when she was ill, she felt a very soothing and comforting female presence—a result of her illness, or a gentle spirit tending to someone that took care of "her" house?

A visitor also reported sensing a spirit in the old barn. The barn was moved to the site in 1975, but it was originally constructed on Verplanck land in Hopewell Junction in the 1720s. The encounter wasn't anything threatening, but the visitor clearly felt that she was not alone.

Over 8,000 years of Native American habitation, three centuries of a Dutch family, and slaves and soldiers can leave quite an impression on property and buildings. Perhaps here at Mount Gulian, history returns to life in many special ways.

Recommendation

Special pieces in the collection include Wappinger Indian beadwork items and the ceremonial pipe marking the sale of the land in 1683, an original badge from the Society of the Cincinnati, and Daniel Verplanck's highchair. Be sure to view the photos of the 1931 fire and the aftermath. Sections of the formal gardens are being restored—from the direct "descendants" of flowers and plants that once grew on the property. Tours provide a greater appreciation for the many interesting people connected with Mount Gulian, and special events offer a wide range of ways to enjoy this site.

Visitor Information

Mount Gulian Historic Site
145 Sterling Street
Beacon, New York 12508
(845) 831-8172
www.mountgulian.org
info@mountgulian.org

A variety of special events are held throughout the season including a military encampment, a colonial dinner, teas, lectures, and holiday season tours. Every October there is a harvest dance in the barn, and scary stories for children. There are also many hands-on educational programs available for school groups.

Admission

Tours of the house, barn, and garden are available on Wednesdays, Thursdays, Fridays, and Sundays from 1 to 5 pm, with the last tour at 4 pm, April 13 to October 31. The fee is $5 for adults; $3 for children (5-15 years of age). Mount Gulian members are free. There are also special events in November and December.

Directions

As listed in their Web site:
Take the Taconic Parkway to Interstate 84 West or take the NY State Thruway to Exit 17 Newburgh to I-84 East. Then take Inerstate-84 to Exit 11 Wappingers Falls/Beacon. Proceed on Route 9D North 2/10^{ths} of a mile. Make left onto Hudson View Drive, and into theHudson View Park Apartments complex, and you will see the Mount Gulian sign. Make an immediate left onto Lamplight Street(which becomes Sterling Street). Pass through the garden apartment complexuntil the end. Mount Gulian is at end of Sterling Street; park on the circular driveway.

The Bottom Line

The History: There is evidence of 8,000 years of Native American habitation on the land. The Verplanck family bought the property in 1683, and the story of their lives is an amazing cross section of the full range of American history. From the earliest settlers in the Hudson Valley, to the Headquarters of Von Steuben, the founding of the Society of the Cincinnati, a runaway slave keeping a journal for forty years, a Civil War officer of U.S. Colored Troops, a devastating act of arson, and subsequent reconstruction. What more could you ask of an historical site?

The Haunting: Ghost sightings are usually fleeting glimpses of shadows, and ghost stories are whispered on dark and stormy nights—except here. During the fire of 1931, numerous credible eyewitnesses clearly saw a man and a woman in colonial-style clothing for a full thirty minutes, and the story was widely reported in newspapers. The presence of other spirits has been sensed in the house and barn.

Four-leafed clovers are supposed to be lucky, but consider this: In the 1960s, the state of New York decided to tear down a house built in 1732, that was one of the critical centers of the Continental Army's operations during the Revolutionary War. And just why was this structure to meet the wrecking ball? So the four entrance and exit ramps of the new Interstate 84 would form a nice, neat cloverleaf!

They say when it comes to real estate, that the three most important things are location, location, location, and that is what helped give the place its important position in history, as well as ultimately putting the house in such a precarious predicament. It was built on the Albany Post Road, the main artery from New York City to Albany, near the Wiccopee Pass. The pass was the only place to easily travel through the surrounding mountains, and it was an ideal location to build fortifications to defend against the British traveling north from Manhattan. (It was also just a short distance to the present-

Van Wyck Homestead

The Van Wyck Homestead Museum in Fishkill.

day Route 52, which at the time was a major route between Boston and Philadelphia.)

In the 1920s, the old post road was updated to Route 9, and planners naturally wanted to create an intersection with this heavily traveled north-south highway and the new east-west Interstate 84. And that put the Van Wyck Homestead in the center of the bull's eye.

Realizing the sheer stupidity of the plans, concerned citizens came together and formed the Fishkill Historical Society in 1962. Thanks to their efforts, they were able to save the house, and the state begrudgingly settled for a two-leafed clover. Of course now, the once-sprawling 959-acre homestead has just one acre in the midst of modern highways and buzzing traffic, but the important thing is that the house and its stories live on.

It was Cornelius Van Wyck who bought this land which was part of the original Rombout Patent. The house was begun in 1732, and when completed, consisted of only three small rooms, which today comprise the lower east wing. The larger main body of the present house was completed around 1757.

Because of the home's ideal location, the Continental Army requisitioned it for use as officers' headquarters, and the land became the site of a very important supply depot and barracks for as many as 2,000 soldiers. The Northern Department Supply Depot operated here from 1776-1783, and every department in the army was represented. It was here that the men were clothed, bread was baked, cannons repaired, horses shod, and tents sewn. There was even that crucial but often overlooked supplier for gentlemen soldiers, the powdered wig maker!

Many famous men spent time here during the Revolution, including Lafayette, Von Steuben, Alexander Hamilton, John Jay, Putnam, and of course, Washington himself. Strategies were planned, orders were given, and much of the paperwork and business of war was conducted. Something else that was conducted here was military court, which leads to two very interesting stories about the place.

For those soldiers who were found guilty for an offense such as stealing, or dereliction of duty, the punishment was generally flogging. There was a huge tree on the property (where Route 9 now runs) where the sentencing was carried out, and the unfortunate soldier would be tied to the tree and whipped the appropriate number of lashes. For generations afterward, the tree was still called the Whipping Tree, but it met its fate in the 1890s when whipping winds toppled it. However, that was not the end of its story.

The mighty tree was cut into lumber, and today in the very room in which the court martials were once held, now stands a table and a box made from the Whipping Tree. There is also another fascinating object on display connected to this tree—literally connected. A massive iron bracket and spikes were found *inside* the tree when it was being cut up. It is believed that this was the bracket to which prisoners were tied to receive their punishments, and over the decades, the huge tree grew around the bracket, finally engulfing it completely!

The other story involves a secret agent, and who doesn't like a good spy mystery? Enoch Crosby was an unlikely hero, a shoemaker by trade who had to leave the regular army due to illness. When a Tory in the area mistakenly took Crosby for a fellow Loyalist, he brought the shoemaker to a secret gathering of Tories who were plotting against the patriots. Crosby managed to sneak away and inform John Jay about the men and their location. The Tories were promptly all rounded up and imprisoned.

Crosby desired to rejoin the regular army, but Jay realized that Crosby had a knack for spying, and persuaded him to act as an American secret agent for several years. He was so successful that only a very few knew the truth about him. So when Crosby was arrested with another group of Tories, in order not to blow his cover, a mock court martial was held at the Van Wyck house. He was found guilty and imprisoned, but arrangements were made for him to "escape" from Fishkill. After the war, he married and went on to lead a long and happy life in the nearby town of Southeast.

This story is remembered primarily because of a novel written by James Fenimore Cooper, entitled, "The Spy." Although Cooper later claimed he never heard of Crosby, there was a connection. Cooper went to school with John Jay's son, and most likely heard of the exciting adventures of the secret, unnamed American spy when visiting the Jay home. Drawing upon Jay's tales of espionage, Enoch Crosby became the character Harvey Birch and the Van Wyck house was called the Wharton House. Fact and fiction eventually melded, and people confused the real with the created. As an example, a postcard on display has a picture of the Van Wyck house, but the caption reads, "The Wharton House!"

When the war was over and the army and wig maker moved on, the Van Wyck's took up residence once again. About 100 years later, the last family member, Sidney Van Wyck, attempted to grow grapes on the property as a new crop. That endeavor failed, as apparently did other things he tried to do in life. While it isn't clear why Sidney became depressed, the end result was that one day he went into the barn and hung himself.

There were other deaths on the property, of soldiers succumbing to the many diseases that struck army camps. The Daughters of the American Revolution placed a monument to these war dead, although the locations of all the graves are not known.

There is one grave on the property that is known, but it is not that of a soldier or a member of the Van Wyck family. In fact, no one even knows who she was or when she died, so how did she end up here?

In the 1970s, a road crew digging on Jackson and Broad Streets in the town of Fishkill unearthed human remains. The skull had a hole in it as if the person had suffered a violent death, and they immediately called the police. It was determined that the skeleton was from an Indian girl, most likely in her teens, and while her death was certainly not a recent crime, she had most likely been killed by whatever penetrated her skull.

While relieved that there wasn't a murderer on the loose, officials were then faced with the dilemma of what to do with the girl's remains. No museums or state agencies were interested, and for quite a while, the bones were driven around Fishkill in the back of the police car. Their next temporary holding place was in the office of the Van Wyck house. Finally, it was decided that she would be reburied under the proposed bicentennial monument.

The Indian girl was quickly forgotten, and until a few years ago, the majority of the current trustees and volunteers had no idea the monument was also a tombstone. To everyone's great surprise, someone mentioned the burial at a meeting, and it was soon decided upon that something more should be done. A Native American group was contacted, and they came and conducted a ceremony for the unknown girl, sanctifying the ground in which she will hopefully now rest in peace.

Apart from the Indian girl, this pyramid-shaped monument is special for another reason. At first glance, it looks like nothing more than a jumble of all colors and manner of odd-shaped stones and pieces of old building material, but there was definite method to this madness.

Rather than just cement a few local stones together to mark the 200th anniversary of the Revolution, it was decided to ask important sites across the country which were involved in the war to send a piece of stone. Thus this unique monument, like America itself, is the result

The bicentennial monument made of stones from many historic sites.

of a combined effort of many people and places. There are over fifty stones from forts and battlefields like Yorktown, Saratoga, and Ticonderoga, as well as pieces of historic buildings. What a clever and wonderful way to acknowledge and pay tribute to all of these sites!

(As a side note—The stones were all mailed to a member of the society, and one day, when he went to the post office to pick up more packages, the clerk strained at the weight and asked, "What do you have in here, rocks?")

With such a long and varied history, are any shades of the past still visible here? While no one has yet reported seeing anything unusual, there have been several instances of inexplicable sounds and footsteps.

One day, two members of the staff—both very credible and reliable teachers—were upstairs when they both clearly heard someone walking around downstairs. There wasn't anything spooky about it, as it was so obviously the footsteps and sounds of a person moving through the rooms and they naturally assumed another staff member or visitor had entered. However, when they went down the stairs to greet whoever it was, they found no one. They even checked outside, but didn't find anyone on the property either, and there were no other cars.

Their story was told to a high-ranking member of the organization, but rather than scoff at the account of the mysterious footsteps, he reinforced it with his own experiences! He stated than on several occasions he has heard someone else in the building, only to find that he was alone, and the doors were locked.

Could it be Sidney Van Wyck who tragically took his own life, or one of the other family members who may have passed here in their 150 years of ownership? Or could it be one of the soldiers who died of disease, or perhaps the Indian girl who met a violent death? Unless someone witnesses a figure or receives some other clue as to the identity of the curious or restless spirit, we won't know. Suffice to say, there is enough evidence to suggest that the historic Van Wyck Homestead continues to be occupied.

Recommendation

If you visit when the house is closed, you can still take a self-guided tour of the property using the brochures kept in a box by the front door. But do try to come when you can have a guided tour of the interior. Look for the table and box made from the Whipping Tree, the bracket found inside, and the photos of the tree before it blew down. Also look for the "Wharton House" postcard. There's a list of all the places that contributed stones to the bicentennial monument. Some of Sidney's grapevines are still growing. Copies of documents detailing the everyday life of the army supply depot are in the military room, and a library of Revolutionary War and Fishkill history is available for use by the public. There's an interesting story behind everything here, so take the time to enjoy it!

Visitor Information

Van Wyck Homestead Museum
504 Route 9
Fishkill, New York 12524
845-896-9560
http://www.fishkillridge.org/history/vanwyck.htm

Hours are Saturday and Sunday, 1 pm to 4 pm from June through October. The Museum and its library are also open by appointment.

Admission

There is no admission fee, but donations are welcomed.
(None of the staff here is paid; they are all volunteers, but obviously the upkeep on an old house is substantial.)

Directions

The Van Wyck Homestead is located in the southeast corner of the intersection of exit 13 of Route 84 and Route 9. The entrance is on Snook Street which is off Route 9, directly across from the eastbound Route 84 exit ramp.

The Bottom Line

The History: Home of an old Dutch family built in 1732 on original Rombout Patent land. Important site of the Northern Department Supply Depot from 1776-1783, headquarters for Continental Army Officers, and a camp for 2,000 soldiers.

The Haunting: Several witnesses on many occasions have heard someone walking around the house.

Section 3

Some ghost stories from the past are so outlandish they are impossible to believe. However, if we pause and ponder what life was like when traveling meant walking or riding on horseback along dark, dangerous roads, we can forgive our ancestors for some of these highly imaginative tales. But what if they did actually see something, and time and retelling eventually distorted the truth of these accounts? The following may be more fancy than fact, or there could be something lurking along the roads of Fishkill…

Animal ghosts are more common than one might think. From beloved cats and dogs who still faithfully search for their masters, to horses who continue to gallop through another world, both ancient legends and modern-day hauntings around the world are filled with animal spirits.

The Hudson Valley may be unique in one respect, however, as it may possess the one and only ghostly pig—an evil ghostly pig, at that. The area this pig was said to haunt was a stretch of the Old Albany Post Road leading north to the town of Fishkill. In fact, this area seemed to possess so many frightening apparitions, both human and animal, that it came to be known as Spook Hollow or Hell Hollow.

South of Fishkill off of Route 9 some of the Old Albany Post Road still exists.

OLD ALBANY POST RD NO

The main concentration of activity on the road took place at Dry Brook, where a short bridge crossed a perilously deep ravine. For over 100 years, travelers were so terrorized by these menacing spirits that they would either refuse to travel along that road at night, or would avoid it completely.

Two human spirits that were often sighted in Dry Brook appeared to be Revolutionary War soldiers. According to historical accounts, there were two unfortunate deaths that did occur in the area during the Revolution. Apparently, twenty American soldiers deserted from the command of General Israel Putnam, due to a lack of food and pay. One deserter attacked an officer trying to stop him. The officer severely wounded the man with his sword, but the soldier still had enough strength to shoot the officer. Both soon died and were buried in a nearby cemetery. Perhaps the nature of their violent deaths caused them to continue to replay the scene in the dead of night along the road. Or perhaps even after death, the soldier continues to search for his freedom and something to eat, while the officer still looks for deserters among those who travel the road.

A more horrifying specter was that of a headless horseman (not to be confused with the *Sleepy Hollow* ghost that Washington Irving made famous). This headless horseman did not appear to be restricted by his obvious handicap, as he used to repeatedly chant "jug-o-rum" while grabbing at the terrified stagecoach travelers who urged their horses to run as if their lives depended upon it (which they just might have). The headless man would attempt to tie his horse to farmer's wagons, or would even jump onto to the wagons, chanting "jug-o-rum" incessantly. There doesn't appear to be any known historical connections that would tie a decapitated, and obviously thirsty, man to that section of road, but it is doubtful anyone ever paused to ask him just what was on his mind.

As frightening as this apparition must have been, the most feared ghost of Spook Hollow seems to have been the pig. It was apparently an enormous hog that would suddenly emerge from the darkness, terrifying the horses and causing them to lose control and race down the road as fast as they could go. Witnesses claimed that the pig appeared as if he wanted to do some kind of harm to the wagons and their drivers.

The most bizarre account of the demon hog came from a stage-coach driver. The driver said that the creature actually broke itself in half. Then the head and front legs of the hog ran in front of his team of terrified horses, while the rear section ran along by the back of the coach. Just before entering the town of Fishkill, both ends of the ghostly pig reunited. There was a very loud sound like a clap of thunder, and then the pig simply vanished into thin air.

The ghosts of Spook Hollow continued their fearful nightly routines up until the 1920s. It was in that decade that the old Albany Post Road underwent considerable changes and eventually became the modern, paved Route 9. Whatever alterations the construction crews made to the area appeared to break the spell of many of the hauntings. Was there some natural force, perhaps emanating from the deep ravine that had acted like some kind of magnet for spiritual energy, drawing to it the tortured souls of both humans and animals? How did the construction of a new road disrupt this energy? Even though Spook Hollow now appears to be free of headless horsemen and demon pigs, it wouldn't be advisable to travel this stretch of road late at night carrying a bottle of rum and a pound of bacon.

Directions

From Route 84, take exit 13 and go south on Route 9, parts of which were the Old Albany Post Road. An original section of the road still exists on your right.

The Bottom Line

The History: The Old Albany Post Road was created to carry mail from New York City to Albany. The road's origins go back to the 1660s, when the Dutch paid Indians to carry letters along their old trails.

The Haunting: If you just can't swallow the tales of a pig ghost and a headless horseman, there are at least the more plausible accounts of the spirits of two Revolutionary War soldiers.

Smalley Inn in Carmel.

Smalley Inn

Smalley Inn in Carmel, New York, may look just like any other small town bar and restaurant, except at Halloween when just about every square inch is covered in spooky decorations. However, even without the decorations, there is something very spooky about the place, and it may very well be one of the most haunted places in the Hudson Valley.

The inn derives its name from James J. Smalley, who bought the hotel in 1852. In addition to running his hotel, he also served at various times as the local sheriff, coroner, and treasurer, until his death in 1867. There is some speculation that the liquor room in the basement was used as a morgue during his stint as coroner, but that has not been corroborated.

The area itself has had some tragic history, including a deadly fire, and the execution of a murderer. Eighteen-year-old George Denny had killed eighty-year-old Abraham Wanzer with a shotgun blast, and on July 26, 1844 at 5 pm, Denny was brought to the gallows erected just across the street and was put to death in front of a crowd of 4,000 people. It was the only hanging in the county's history, and obviously a very popular event.

Technically, however, the statement that it was the county's only hanging is incorrect, if we also consider suicide by hanging. One day, a woman came into Smalley's with a newspaper clipping that described the death of a family member a couple of generations earlier. The man had hung himself, in a second floor room at Smalley's!

Anthony Porto began operating Smalley's in 1968 as a restaurant and tavern. His son, Tony, Jr., has been managing the place for the last twenty years. While there were already strange things happening, activity really picked up when a friend brought over a Ouija board and asked if any spirits were present. The board spelled out a name that only Tony knew—it was the name of a former employee who had also committed suicide.

From that day, there has been an almost endless succession of sightings, sounds, and inexplicable phenomena. The following are just some of the highlights:

Crying Child

There are sightings of a little girl in an old fashioned dress, "like a *Little House on the Prairie* dress," and people have heard a child crying or laughing. That activity began when a tombstone was found nearby and stored in the basement—the tombstone of Elizabeth Smalley, who had died in the mid-1800s at the age of seven.

Basement Woes

Tony wanted to have some renovations done in the basement, so he hired a man to remove one of the original brick pillars, which was right by the basement stairs where the tombstone was kept. After working for just a short time, the man quit because he claimed that someone kept pushing him into the pile of bricks. Another man was hired, but he quit after claiming that as he worked someone kept pulling on his shirt. Finally, a third man was hired. He simply ran out, saying he just couldn't work down there. In fact, he left so suddenly that he didn't even take his tools—and he refused to come back to Smalley's to get them.

Stranger Than Fiction

One night, every cell phone and house phone in the place started ringing at exactly the same time, although no one actually placed the calls.

Employees have gotten trapped inside the meat locker which can only be locked from the outside.

Footsteps are heard when no one else is in the building.

People feel their clothes being tugged.

Doors slam shut, and locked doors are found open.

The juke box turns on and plays music even when it is unplugged.

Employees and patrons have claimed to see strange images in the large mirror in the front dining area.

The experiences here are widespread and numerous, and while most apt to occur at night, can happen any time of day, anywhere inside the building. Old hotels have often witnessed a lot of tragedies and intense human emotions that can leave lasting impressions. Try visiting Smalley's for yourself, and see if it makes an impression on you!

Recommendation

After a long day of ghost touring, this is the perfect spot to relax and enjoy the food and drinks. But don't relax too much—there may be something happening at any time in Smalley's.

Visitor Information

Smalley Inn
57 Main Street
(Also known as Gleneida Avenue and Route 52)
Carmel, New York, 10512
845-225-4007

Hours: 11:30 am to 3 am, 7 days a week
Family restaurant featuring Italian and American cuisine.

Directions

From I-84: At exit 18, turn onto ramp towards RT 311/Lake Carmel/Patterson. In one mile, turn right (west) onto SR-311. In three miles, turn left (south) onto SR-52, which is also called Gleneida Avenue and Main Street in the town of Carmel. Smalley Inn is at #57 on your right.

The Bottom Line

The History: A building from the 1800s that has operated as a hotel, restaurant, and bar. A hanging took place across the street, and a suicide occurred in the building.

The Haunting: A little girl is seen in an old-fashioned dress. People are tugged and pushed, electronics go haywire, footsteps, and other sounds are heard.

Everyone knows Stonehenge, the most recognizable megalithic site in the world. Mysterious ancient stone structures have always fascinated both archeologists and the general public, and around the world such sites are protected and studied—except, unfortunately, for those sites in the Hudson Valley. Most people don't even know of the existence of the stone chambers that number in the hundreds. Archeologists don't view them as worthy of preservation, and many chambers have already been lost to the bulldozers of developers.

The "expert" archaeological view is that they are all colonial root cellars and not even worth a second look—and this opinion is often given by professionals who haven't even looked at them once! (In any science, it does help if you actually examine something *before* rendering an opinion.) On the other end of the spectrum are the wild theories about the builders and functions of the chambers, with speculation ranging from an alien connection, to unknown ancient civilizations with all manner of mystical purposes ascribed to them.

Setting aside both extremes, what can be reasonably concluded from examining the facts? Root cellars are generally just that, cellars dug into the ground for storing vegetables. The stone chambers are at ground level, with corbelled stone walls with massive stone slab ceilings. Would colonists have built their homes with timber, and then exerted an enormous amount of time and energy moving huge stones just to store potatoes?

Stone Chambers

Magnetic anomalies have been found at chamber sites. Whoever built them had some knowledge about the Earth's magnetic fields, and felt it was important to place the chambers at such places. Also, many of the stone chambers are aligned to astronomical events, such as the solstices and equinoxes. Do potatoes care if they are stored in magnetic fields in alignment with the vernal equinox?

Clearly, these structures cannot all be dismissed as colonial root cellars, but does that mean they have some alien origins? Obviously, any group of ordinary people is capable of stacking stones, but the construction methods and alignments do suggest an organized society with some advanced knowledge. Native Americans would have had the ability, and even though they were not known in recent history to build in stone in the Hudson Valley, that doesn't preclude their ancestors from having done so.

We also know that Columbus was not the first European to reach the shores of North America. Vikings, Celts, possibly even the ancient Phoenicians may have crossed the Atlantic. Could some other group of people long ago have constructed these stone chambers? Perhaps, but until serious archeological work is done, we can only hope the chambers remain intact for future study.

The question now arises, why do people assign mystical qualities to these small stone structures? The reason is because there have been many eyewitness accounts of strange phenomena, not the least of which have been seeing the figures of Vikings and hooded monks in and around the chambers. There have also been numerous reports of glowing lights inside the chambers, as well as lights moving around and above the outside of the structures. Many people have also reported feeling light headed and disoriented inside some of the chambers, as if some strange force was affecting them.

Could the Earth's magnetic fields or some other natural forces be responsible for the lights and strange feelings? Possibly, but even if these sites induced some type of hallucinations, why would different people at different times all see Vikings or hooded monks?

At the very least, the stone chambers of the Hudson Valley are lightning rods for controversy. From the archeologists who refuse to even look at them, to those who speculate wildly about their origins, these sites evoke strong reactions. Whether you call them root cellars or star chambers, they are tangible reminders that there are still mysteries in this world, some of which are in our own backyards.

Recommendation

Here's your chance to play Indiana Jones for a day. Visit a few stone chambers, bring your camera, tape measure, compass (to check alignments), and an EMF meter (instruments used to measure electromagnetic fields) and conduct your own field investigation. Some chambers are on private property, so don't trespass. There are some chambers right on the road you can drive up to, and many others that require a hike. Be sure to check them out both during the day to get a good look at them and take photos, and at night when strange things are supposed to happen and lights are seen.

Visitor Information

A well-preserved chamber adjacent to the road is on Route 301 in Kent Cliffs, just a few hundred feet to the south of the intersection of Farmers Mills Road, also known as Route 42. It's on the right side as you're heading south, and clearly visible in the fall and winter, but in spring and summer can be somewhat camouflaged by the leaves, so look closely. Another chamber is just to 0.6 miles to the west on Route 301, directly across from Forest Court. That chamber is easily seen all year.

You can hike to the King's Chamber (so called because it's the largest in Putnam County) and its standing stone in Clarence Fahnestock State Park. It is located to the south of where the Taconic and Pudding Street intersect. You can obtain a trail map and directions at the park headquarters on Route 301, just west of the Taconic exit. There are other sites in the park so it's worth exploring.

There are many other stone chambers scattered throughout the area on Peekskill Hollow Road, Oscawana Lake Road, John Simpson Road, Reservoir Road, Lower Magnetic Mine Road, Ludington Road, and Gypsy Trail Road, to name a few. Drive slowly and keep a sharp lookout.

The Bottom Line

The History: Are the stone chambers colonial root cellars, or are they thousands of years old? Theories as to who built them range from Native Americans, to Vikings, to Celts, to Phoenicians, to some unknown ancient civilization. They just may be the oldest structures in the Hudson Valley.

The Haunting: People have seen the figures of Vikings and hooded monks in and around the chambers. There have also been many eyewitness accounts of glowing and flashing lights in, around, and high above the chambers. People have felt odd and disoriented inside the chambers.

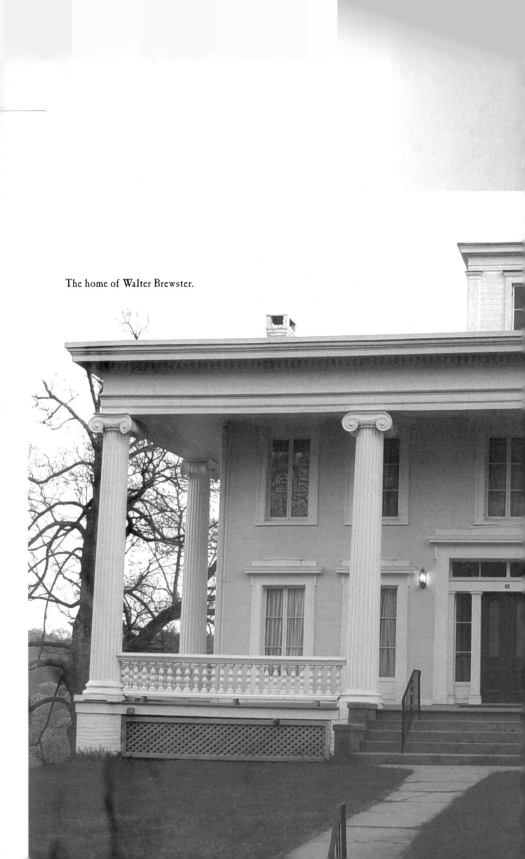

The home of Walter Brewster.

Walter Brewster House

Due to nineteenth-century fires and twentieth-century "progress," not much remains of the original Village of Brewster, which was incorporated in 1848. The village began when the enterprising Walter Brewster and his brother, James, bought 134 acres of farmland, then arranged for the railroad to stop on their property. A community of houses grew around the new train station, and in 1850, the founder of the village needed a suitable home of his own, and one that reflected his success and status.

Fortunately, that house has survived, although at times, it appeared destined for the wrecking ball, but more on that in a moment. First, there is another owner who needs to be acknowledged—John Gail Borden, the son of Gail Borden, the famous founder of the Borden dairy, which spawned the even more famous Elsie the Cow advertising mascot. Gail Borden had built a factory in Brewster in 1863 to process and can the 80,000 quarts of milk produced every day by local Putnam County cows.

After the Bordens, the house had a variety of uses as apartments, a temporary school, and the home of the Knights of Columbus. It was then vacant for many years, and what was left of the original structure after extensive remodeling, vandalism, and decay, presented a forlorn picture. But thanks to the Landmarks Preservation Society of Southeast, private donations, and thirty years of hard work, the house is once again a place that the founder of Brewster would have been proud to call home.

The question remains, however, that while the structure has been brought back to life, does anything else there try to reconnect with the world of the living? As no one occupies the old bedrooms or sits quietly with a good book in the parlor, it's difficult to say if any Brewsters or Bordens have yet to leave the premises, but there have been some reports that when the house is empty, the lights have gone on and off, and curtains have been pulled back as if someone was peering out. Maybe things do go bump in the night here, and the spirits are just waiting for someone to notice.

Recommendation

A pleasant surprise when driving through the surrounding nondescript suburban homes. Not open to the public on a regular basis, the house can be seen and enjoyed during one of the special events, tours, or concerts.

Visitor Information

Walter Brewster House
43 Oak Street
Brewster, New York 10509
(845) 279-7429

Call for information on tours and concerts. There are also living history programs and holiday events.

Directions

From I-84: At exit 19, turn west onto SR-312. In one mile, turn east onto US-6. In 2.1 miles, bear left onto Oak Street. The Brewster House is 0.3 miles ahead on your right.

The Bottom Line

The History: The magnificent Greek Revival style home of the founder of the Village of Brewster. Also owned by John Gail Borden of Borden's dairies.

The Haunting: When the house is empty, lights go on and off, and curtains are pulled back as it someone is peering out.

The small island in the Hudson River where Bannerman built his castle.

In Dutchess County there is a rocky little island in the Hudson River—an island whose size belies its wealth of history. Though not quite seven acres, this piece of land contains hundreds of years of lore and legend, as well as a literally explosive recent past.While its official name is Pollopel Island, it is popularly known as Bannerman's Island, thanks to the entrepreneur who built a castle on it early in the twentieth century. Castles are often viewed as prime haunting territory, but this island was considered haunted long before a single stone was set in place.

Bannerman's Castle

Bannerman's Castle.

By the time the Dutch arrived in the Hudson Valley in the 1600s, Pollopel Island already had a long-standing reputation. The Indians in the area believed it to be haunted, and even those brave enough to venture to the island in daylight would never set foot on it at night. This made it an ideal place for the Dutch to seek refuge whenever the prospect of hostilities with the Indians arose. Yet even though at first they looked to the island as a place of safety, they too, came to regard it as being haunted.

In addition to a belief in evil spirits, the Dutch believed there were also evil goblins who were led by the worst goblin of all, the Heer of Dunderberg. These goblins were supposed to be responsible for causing storms and strong winds that made river navigation treacherous. As if this wasn't enough to scare sailors on their first journey upriver, the Dutch used to get these new sailors drunk and leave the poor terrified men on the island while they completed their business to the north. On the way back, they would pick up the sailors who had hopefully conquered their fears during their brief stay on the island.

Early in the eighteenth century, a ship called the *Flying Dutchman* was carrying passengers up the river to Fishkill. Whether caused by the angry Heer of Dunderberg, or simply by the volatile valley weather, a terrible storm arose as the ship approached Pollopel Island. The captain of the ship tried his best to save his vessel and all the lives aboard, but the storm overwhelmed the *Flying Dutchman*. The ship sank just to the south of Pollopel, resulting in a terrible loss of life.

From the time of that tragedy, generations of fisherman and sailors claimed to hear strange things in the waters around the island. During storms, they believed they could hear the phantom captain of the *Flying Dutchman* still shouting his desperate commands to the long-dead crew, and the cries of the victims of the shipwreck. The presence of this local ghost ship must have gone far to enhance the aura of mystery and fear about the island.

During the Revolutionary War, the British were of far greater concern to the locals than spirits. The waters near Pollopel were obstructed by chains and spiked posts in an attempt to prevent British warships from gaining control of the river. George Washington issued orders calling for buildings to be constructed on the island to house munitions and prisoners, although it is not certain if these projects were ever completed. In the more tranquil postwar years, the island became a spot for recreation and a kind of outpost for fishermen.

Over a hundred years later, Pollopel Island would return to military purposes, although in a rather unique way. The Scottish immigrant Francis Bannerman bought the island in 1900 to house his vast inventory of firearms, ammunition, and equipment. By buying huge quantities of army surplus, Bannerman had made himself the foremost dealer of these military goods, selling both by catalog and from his store in New York City. Not only did Pollopel provide the perfect location to store his stockpile of weapons (New York officials were not keen on the idea of Bannerman's enormous amounts of gun powder being stored in the heart of the city), it gave Bannerman the opportunity of using his growing wealth to build his dream home, or dream castle, as the case may be.

Based upon authentic Scottish castles, Bannerman himself designed the huge stone home, as well as the storehouses and other buildings. To facilitate the construction of docks and breakwaters, Bannerman bought aging ships and had them sunk along the shore and covered with concrete.

One tugboat captain who had been very fond of his vessel had asked Bannerman if he would please tell the workmen that before they sank it, they make sure that he was far enough down river so that he didn't have to witness his beloved ship's demise. Either the request was not forwarded to the workmen, or they didn't take it seriously, because just as the captain was departing the island, the tugboat was sunk right before his eyes.

The captain, infuriated by what he considered to be a personal affront, shook his fist and hurled curses at Bannerman. He swore that he would return, that Bannerman had not heard the last of this old captain. While it's doubtful that anyone at the time took him seriously, there is a chance that the angry captain's threats turned out to be more than just mere words.

A lodge was built on the site of the sunken ship and in its basement was a workshop. For years, employees down in the workshop claimed to hear the ringing of a ship's bell beneath them, where the old tugboat bell would have been. It was the distinct double ringing that a ship used to signal that it was going in reverse. The belief soon arose that the spirit of the angry captain had returned and that he was trying to reverse his ship and get it away from the island.

Notwithstanding the ghostly captain's efforts, the tugboat remained, construction continued, and the storehouses were completed and filled. Francis Bannerman died in 1918, but his family continued the lucrative business. However, not all was to be peace and quiet on Bannerman's Island. There were several accidents over the years, accidents which are to be expected handling vast amounts of live ammunition and powder.

However, in 1920 there was one unexpected explosion of massive proportions. The blast was so powerful that it propelled a stone wall over a thousand feet across the river and onto the eastern shore, creating a large obstruction on the train tracks. Windows were shattered for miles around. Pieces of buildings, as well as pieces of the island itself, were hurled into the water.

Despite the terrible destruction, the business survived and continued on for another fifty years. However, the family decided to move its storehouses to a more convenient location on Long Island. The Bannermans continued ownership of the castle and island until 1968, when the entire property was sold to the state of New York. There were plans for restoring the castle and turning the island into a park, but the real death blow came the following year. A fire broke out, decimating the castle and other buildings.

In the years before this disaster, caretakers and their families did live happily on the island. Yet on many occasions, strange things occurred to remind the occupants of the mysterious reputation of the place. Many times late at night, the sound of a horse running across the drawbridge could plainly be heard. There was only one small problem with this—there were no horses on Bannerman's Island!

There was also a strange whistling sound that could be heard moving around the island. It was an odd, high-pitched whistling sound for which no one could ever find a source. This, combined with the ringing bell, ghost captain, and phantom horse, helped to insure that the ancient Indian beliefs that the island was haunted would be perpetuated for generations to come.

Recommendation

If you are thinking of kayaking or canoeing out to the island on your own, think again. There are deceptively strong currents around the island and the remaining stone walls could collapse at any time, not to mention the snakes, biting insects, and poison ivy.

Efforts are underway by The Bannerman Castle Trust to raise money to stabilize the structures and restore the walkways, and guided tours are available on weekends. (See visitor information below.)

Visitor Information

Bannerman's Island and his castle can be seen from various locations along the riverbank, and by looking south from the Newburgh-Beacon Bridge, but for more than a glimpse and for the opportunity to take pictures, stop at one of the parking areas along Route 9D between Cold Spring and Beacon. The best location is the parking area located 0.2 miles north of the tunnel. Cross the railroad tracks to the river and look north. Binoculars or a zoom lens on your camera will give your best view. *Be very careful of the passing trains.*

Go to www.bannermancastle.org for information regarding on-island boat tours, off-island boat tours, and kayak/canoe trips.

Note: Contributions and inquiries to The Bannerman Castle Trust can be directed to info@bannermancastle.org or (845)-831-6346.

The Bottom Line

The History: Native Americans were afraid of this island, so the early Dutch settlers used it to seek refuge during times of trouble. Soldiers, mariners, and fisherman have used the place for centuries. The most famous occupant was Francis Bannerman, who built a castle on the island and ran his surplus military goods business there. A massive explosion and a later fire destroyed the buildings, except for the stone walls.

The Haunting: Long before the Dutch arrived in the 1600s, the Native Americans thought this island was haunted. There are hundreds of years of stories and legends of strange happenings here, including the spirits of shipwreck victims crying out for help, a phantom horse running across the island, an angry captain ringing the bell of his sunken ship, and a inexplicable whistling sound.

In 1961, Governor Nelson Rockefeller referred to Boscobel as "one of the most beautiful homes ever built in America." It is also a home that has undergone the most amazing journeys, both figuratively and literally. It was originally constructed on a site fifteen miles away, was abandoned and stripped of many key features, faced total destruction twice, then, at the last minute, was salvaged and pieced back together on its present location in Garrison, New York. If ever a historic house has faced adversity and triumphed due to the perseverance of many dedicated individuals, it is Boscobel.

The journey of one of America's most beautiful homes began with a man loyal to the British during the Revolutionary War, who may actually have had the architectural plans drawn up in England. States Morris Dyckman (1755-1806) was descended from one of the earliest Dutch families to settle in New Amsterdam (which was to become New York City) in the 1600s. During the war he was a clerk for the British Army's Quartermaster Department, and after the war he made a fortune from several wealthy men he helped to clear from charges of abusing their posts by profiteering. Some money was freely given in gratitude for his services, but it was basically extortion that forced others to pay hush money to Dyckman.

Boscobel

The beautiful tree-lined entrance to Boscobel.

As States Dyckman enjoyed a high standard of living—and wished to openly display his refined taste—these ill-gotten gains helped to realize his vision of a magnificent home befitting a country gentleman. In 1804, construction began in Montrose, New York, at a location overlooking Haverstraw Bay. Unfortunately, Dyckman didn't live to see his dream mansion completed, as he died in August of 1806. The elegant Federal-style house was finally finished in 1808 and occupied by his widow, Elizabeth Corné Dyckman, and their young son, Peter (they also had a daughter, Letitia, born in 1799, but she died).

Elizabeth was the eighteen-year-old granddaughter of a wealthy Loyalist when she married the thirty-nine-year-old States. She was a beautiful woman who proved capable of handling all the affairs of both the house and surrounding farmland. She also managed to care for State's mother and sister during their final illnesses, while raising Peter, as well as an illegitimate son States had fathered with another woman before his marriage to Elizabeth. She succumbed to an illness in 1823 at the age of forty-seven, and her son died the following year at the young age of twenty-seven.

Boscobel remained in the family until 1888. After a series of owners, the house was acquired by Westchester County and was to be developed as a park. The first threat to the house's existence came in 1941 when it was announced that it would be demolished. An organization of concerned individuals was quickly formed and they managed to raise enough funds to keep the structure standing.

The next owner was the Veterans Administration who purchased the Montrose property in order to build a hospital. In the greatest indignity suffered by this stately home, in 1955 the VA sold the "useless" building for the paltry sum of $35! The contractor who bought the abandoned structure stripped away most of the fine decorative molding from the interior and exterior, then prepared to demolish what was left.

Once again, determined citizens sprang into action and the remaining pieces of the house were stored in garages, barns, and basements in hopes that money could someday be raised to find a new site on which to reconstruct this historic treasure. Thanks primarily to Mrs. Lila Acheson Wallace (who had founded the *Reader's Digest* with her husband), land was purchased at a site in Garrison with breathtaking views of the Hudson River. Much of the molding was recovered and the house was reassembled. With seemingly more lives than a cat, Boscobel was opened to the public on May 21, 1961, for future generations to enjoy.

However, more changes were to come. Great pains had been taken to furnish the home in the manner they assumed States had been accustomed to on his lengthy trips abroad, i.e., with English furniture. They also chose color schemes, floor coverings, and wallpapers they thought suited the structure. However, in 1975 after the discovery of an 1806 household inventory and further research into other documentation and Dyckman family heirlooms, it became apparent that historical accuracy had suffered for the sake of esthetic interpretation.

Boscobel once again closed its doors while the interiors were all redone, and American furnishings—such as those of Duncan Phyfe and other New York City cabinetmakers and craftsmen—were purchased to recreate what would have been historically correct for the period when Elizabeth lived there. Original English china and glass purchased by States are also part of the current collection, which all combines into an incomparable showpiece of decorative arts in a magnificent home in a stunning river-view setting.

States Dyckman, staunch British Loyalist, truly has as his legacy one of the most beautiful of American homes.

Obviously, recent generations have loved this house enough to put enormous amounts of time and effort into rescuing, restoring and preserving it, but is its considerable charm strong enough to still attract generations from the past? Indications are that Boscobel does still retain impressions, if not the actual spirits, of those who first loved this place in a distant time and in another location.

When well-known Hudson Valley psychic Lisa Ann visited Boscobel, she saw a woman standing on the side of the large palladium window at the back of the house, and felt that the woman was the wife of the original owner. She felt that others must have seen her, and after some research it was discovered that there had been another witness—a former caretaker of the property.

One November afternoon, the man finished locking up the mansion for the day and walked to his truck parked at the back of the house. For some reason he looked up at the window and was stunned to see a beautiful woman looking down at him, slowly waving her hand, standing exactly in the spot where Lisa Ann had seen her. He knew it was Elizabeth Dyckman, because she appeared just as she looks in her portrait which hangs in the house. Even though it was an understandably frightening experience, he felt that Elizabeth was simply thanking him for all his efforts in taking good care of "her house."

Does States Dyckman still sit in Boscobel's lovely dining room?

Lisa Ann also sensed the presence of a "somber man" in the dining room, who was contemplating some anniversary. She felt he was the original owner, but at the time, she was unaware that States Dyckman didn't live to see his dream home built, or that it was the 200th anniversary of the completion of Boscobel. Perhaps the home States was sadly denied in life, he now ruefully contemplates in death?

The Dyckmans will always be inexorably tied to Boscobel, whether it is in spirit or simply from the legacy of their vision and determination. They embraced the finest architecture and decorative arts of the period and created a world of elegance in a rural Hudson Valley setting. In the twentieth century, that vision was almost obliterated, but fortunately, we can still marvel at the beauty both within the house and throughout the grounds. And if in the hustle and bustle of the new century we linger to take in these wonderful sights of a quieter time long gone, could we blame those who made this all possible for lingering, as well?

Recommendation

There are some massive mansions along the Hudson, but none can compare with the simple elegance of Boscobel. The fine collection of furnishings and antiques, presented in authentic period settings, brings a warm, rich dimension that isn't possible in a museum.

Be sure when you take the guided tour to set aside enough time to enjoy the grounds, which are equally spectacular when spring is in bloom, when autumn has set the Hudson Valley ablaze with color, or when the snows of winter seem to place a gentle silence across the landscape. Whether you visit during their famous Shakespeare Festival to watch a play beneath the summer stars, or take a candlelight tour at Christmastime, Boscobel is a place worth visiting every season of the year.

Visitor Information

Boscobel Restoration, Inc.
1601 Route 9D, Garrison, New York 10524
Phone 845-265-3638   Fax: 845-265-4405
info@boscobel.org
www.boscobel.org

Boscobel is open every day except Tuesdays, Thanksgiving, and Christmas. The museum and grounds are closed to the public January, February and March. There is a Museum Shop located in the Carriage House Reception Center that features Hudson Valley history, horticulture, and nature, as well as gift items and books.

Hours

April through October: 9:30 am to 5 pm (last tour begins at 4:15 pm). November and December: 9:30 am to 4 pm (last tour begins at 3:15 pm.

Admission

Adults, $15; Seniors (62 and older), $12; Children (ages 6-14), $7; Children under age 6 admitted free. Grounds Only: Adults $8, Children (ages 6-14) $5, Children under age 6 admitted free. *Special rates are available for groups of 12 or more and for school groups.*

Special events

Boscobel offers an amazing variety of events and presentations from Shakespeare to jazz, astronomy, high tea, and turtle walks. Separate admissions may be charged for special events. Check the events calendar on their Web site for dates and information.

Three popular annual events are:

—The Hudson Valley Shakespeare Festival presents plays on the lawn of Boscobel from June through August.

—The Annual Snapping Turtle Walk is in early-to-mid June and is held in conjunction with staff members of the National Audubon Society's Constitution Marsh Sanctuary, and includes a guided walk around the grounds in search of female turtles laying their eggs.

—The Traditional Candlelight Tour is held Friday, Saturday, and Sunday in mid-December when Boscobel is illuminated by hundreds of candles and decorated with beautiful natural hand-made decorations. There is live classical music, and you can enjoy a toast from Boscobel's wassail bowl and a taste of delicious fruitcake.

Directions

As listed on their Web site: http://www.boscobel.org/directions.html

From Westchester: Taconic State Parkway north to the Cold Spring, Route 301 west exit. Take Route 301 into the Village of Cold Spring. Turn left at the traffic light at the intersection with 9D, and follow 9D south for one mile. Boscobel is clearly marked on the right.

From Manhattan and New Jersey: Upper level George Washington Bridge to Palisades Parkway north to Bear Mt. Bridge to Route 9D.

From Long Island: Throgs Neck or Whitestone Bridge to I-287 to Taconic State Parkway north. Taconic to the Cold Spring, Route 301 west exit. Take Route 301 into the village of Cold Spring. Turn left at the traffic light at the intersection with Route 9D and follow south for one mile. Boscobel is clearly marked on the right.

From the North: NY Thruway to I-84 east; cross the Newburgh-Beacon Bridge to Route 9D south, exit 11, and drive eleven miles south to Boscobel.

Or...

Taconic State Parkway south to the Cold Spring, Route 301 west exit. Take Route 301 into the village of Cold Spring. Turn left at the traffic light at the intersection with Route 9D and follow south for one mile. Boscobel is clearly marked on the right.

From points West: I-84 east across the Newburgh-Beacon Bridge to Route 9D south, exit 11. Drive eleven miles south to Boscobel.

The Bottom Line

The History: How many other mansions can you name that were saved from destruction, taken apart piece by piece, and reconstructed fifteen miles away? The history of the Dyckman family is fascinating, and the story of Boscobel's survival is amazing.

The Haunting: States Dyckman sits silently in the dining room he never saw completed, while Elizabeth stands by the palladium window to keep watch over her property.

It sounds like something out of an Alfred Hitchcock movie—a woman overhears her husband plotting to murder her. She runs for her life into the darkness of a cold winter's night. She makes it to the train station, where the 10:15 pm local to Poughkeepsie will carry her to the safety of her brother's house.

Sitting nervously on the bench in the waiting room, she listens as the clock ticks slowly. Only two minutes to go, only two minutes to safety…but too late. At 10:13 pm, her husband finds her and stabs her to death. To this day, the murdered woman's spirit is said to haunt this station.

Unfortunately, this was not a movie plot, it was a very real crime committed at the Cold Spring Depot in 1898. The first depot was a simple wooden structure built in 1849. When that burned down in the 1880s, a new brick building was constructed by Cornelius Vanderbilt. The station remained active until 1954, when the building was sold to a Jeep dealer. The place then became a restaurant in 1972.

The present owner, Tom Rolston, bought the place in 1985, and very soon after, he and his business partner discovered that there may be some truth to the ghostly legend. While the story stated that anyone sitting on the bench in the waiting room at 10:13 pm would feel the cold chill of the woman's spirit,

The Cold Spring Depot restaurant.

even after the bloodstained bench was removed and the waiting room was redesigned, odd things still happened. Locked doors would be opened, lights would turn on, and any toilet seat that was left up the night before would be found down the next morning (which Rolston points out, proves the ghost is that of a woman!).

There has never been anything threatening, but clearly the spirit of the woman wanted people aware of her presence, and wanted her tragic story to be known. Today, every patron can read about the crime on the restaurant's placemats while sitting in the dining room, which was the original waiting room where the murder occurred. Or, if you prefer some fresh air, you can dine outside and watch the dozens of trains that whiz by every day, at speeds of 115 mph, and you can imagine what it was like waiting for the 10:15 to arrive. Whatever choice you make, the Cold Spring Depot certainly offers more exciting experiences than your average restaurant!

Recommendation

While the Cold Spring Depot is a great place to eat any time of year, it's wonderful to be able to sit outside and enjoy the park and the trains in warmer weather. And on a hot summer's day, be sure to get some of their ice cream to take with you if you plan a stroll around town.

Visitor Information

Cold Spring Depot
1 Depot Square
Cold Spring, New York 10516
845-265-5000
www.coldspringdepot.com

The restaurant is open 7 days a week from 11 am to 11 pm. The Ice Cream Parlor is open May through November.

Directions

As listed on their Web site:

From New York State Thruway: Thruway Exit 17 (Newburgh) to I-84 East, cross Newburgh-Beacon Bridge; and continue to I-84 Exit 13, turn right from exit ramp onto Route 9 South, then continue 6.5 miles to light at Route 301, turn right. Continue 2.4 miles to traffic light at Route 9D, and downhill, straight thru light. At the bottom of the hill (at railroad tracks) turn right onto Depot Square and park.

From the Palisades Parkway: Palisades Parkway north to Bear Mountain exit (right), and continue to the Bear Mountain traffic circle at Route 9W, exiting traffic circle to Bear Mountain Bridge. Left turn after crossing bridge, continue on Route 9D north for 8.3 miles to village of Cold Spring, turn left at the village traffic light, onto Main Street. Go to the bottom of Main Street (at the railroad tracks) turn right on Depot Square and park.

From the Taconic Parkway: Taconic State Parkway in Putnam County to the Route 301 exit (signs at this exit are also marked for: Cold Spring and Carmel). If traveling south on the Taconic, turn right from the exit ramp; and if traveling north on the Taconic, turn left from the exit ramp; continue west on Route 301 for 8 miles to traffic light at Route 301 and Route 9. Continue straight through light for 2.4 miles, to next traffic light (Route 9D), go straight on Main Street to the bottom of the hill (at the railroad tracks) turn right on Depot Square and park.

The Bottom Line

The History: A train station built by Cornelius Vanderbilt in the 1880s, and the site of a notorious murder in 1898.

The Haunting: The spirit of a murdered woman still makes her presence known.

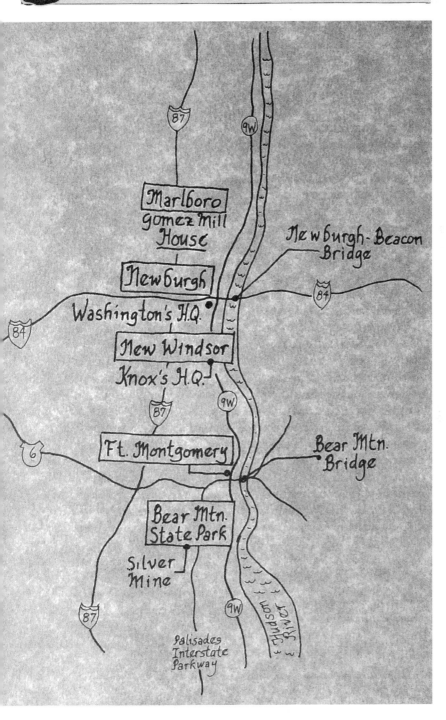

The Gomez Mill House in Marlboro.

Gomez Mill House

The story of this historic site begins in Spain in 1660, when Luis Moses Gomez was born into a wealthy Jewish family with close ties to the royal court. Life should have been good for the boy, but due to the Spanish Inquisition, the family was forced to flee to France. Over the next forty years, Luis Gomez traveled far and wide, finally settling in New York City.

The Gomez family soon became the richest and most influential Jewish family in America at the time, but Luis was not content to rest on his fortune. In 1714, he bought 6,000 acres of land on the banks of the Hudson River so he could build an Indian trading post.

Ironically, the land included a former Indian ceremonial site known as the Danskammer. (The Dutch, frightened by the sight of a large Indian ceremony held there one night, called it "de Dans Kamer van de Duyfel"—the "Devil's Dance Chamber.") When the trading post was built, the Indians returned to the land that they once held sacred to trade furs in exchange for trinkets, guns, and rum.

However, both the dwindling Indian and fur-bearing animal populations made the trading post obsolete in thirty years. The simple one-room trading post with its three-foot thick walls was to undergo several expansions over the centuries in the hands of some interesting owners. Wolvert Acker, a staunch patriot and member of the Ulster County Militia, bought the place in 1772, and added a second story and a large attic, using bricks made on site. In 1835, the Armstrong family purchased the property, and Edward Armstrong added a fine mansion on the Danskammer overlooking the river.

In general, life was very good for the wealthy, talented, and adventurous Armstrong family, but one poignant tragedy hung like a dark cloud over their lives. In 1873, the bright and energetic five-year-old Emily Armstrong was playing near the mill creek in front of the house. She had been running with her dog, Twist, when she fell and hit her head on a rock. Her lifeless body was found face down in the creek, and legend has it that Twist died shortly after of a broken heart. Though the family lived there for another thirty years, they never fully recovered from their terrible loss.

The next owner was craftsman Dard Hunter, who built a quaint-looking paper mill on the creek. He would make his handmade paper in the mill, then hang the sheets to dry in the attic. The Hunters attracted an artistic crowd, and many famous people, including furniture designer Gustav Stickley, regularly visited the old mill house.

The last family, and arguably the most important private owners since Luis Gomez, bought the place after World War II, when America entered a baby and building boom. Historic structures were being torn down for new housing developments, and Mildred Starin didn't want to see that happen to this magnificent house. Her philosophy was that while "striving for the new, we should cherish and protect the old," and through her efforts, the Gomez Mill House was preserved and protected by entering it into the National Register of Historic Places in 1973.

Mildred also contacted family members of former owners, and brought back many important pieces of these families' histories to the house, such as Wolvert Acker's Bible box, documents, paintings, and artifacts. The second part of her plan was to open the house to the public, which was accomplished when the Gomez Mill Foundation was formed and bought the property in 1984.

Today, the oldest Jewish residence in America, and the home of patriots, entrepreneurs, adventurers, artists, and preservationists is open to the public for tours, lectures, classes, and events. It may also have an open door to the other world…

The following highlights just some of the eyewitness accounts of unexplained activity in the house and on the property:

Swinging Doors

A member of the staff was cleaning the main staircase, when suddenly the door beneath the stairs swung open. She came down the stairs and closed it, but it forcefully swung open again. Stepping back, she looked up at the stairs, and there, right in front of her, was the face of a small boy with an old-fashioned Dutch boy haircut, peering at her from between the balusters of the railing.

Rocking Horse

A member of the staff was alone cleaning the upstairs bedroom of a former owner who once ran a school in the house. As she was about to exit the room she saw that the antique rocking horse in the hall was rocking back and forth. She looked on in disbelief as the horse moved on its own, and she could have sworn she heard a child

Emily Armstrong's rocking horse.
Young Emily tragically lost her life on the property in 1873.

laughing. Then, just as she crossed the threshold from the bedroom into the hall, the horse abruptly stopped moving and became perfectly still, as if a hand had stopped it. This rocking horse had belonged to Emily Armstrong, who tragically lost her life on the property in 1873.

Fire Hazards

Several years ago there was a fire, and the firemen who responded claimed that the place was haunted, as something frightening happened to them when they were inside that they didn't want to talk about. Apparently it was no joke, as they later went to a priest to get blessed and sprinkled with holy water. To this day, one of the firemen still refuses to set foot back in the house. (It should be pointed out that he was also a prominent local politician, with nothing to gain by spreading stories of ghosts.)

Babies, Smoke and Voices

A nun who was walking the grounds reported seeing the spirits of two babies over the millpond.

Cigar smoke has often been smelled in certain rooms, although for years there has been a strict no smoking rule.

Voices of a man and woman speaking loudly have been heard by the mill.

Swinging Lights

Several staff members observed the light fixture in the kitchen swinging back and forth. One woman took hold of it and stopped the motion. A few minutes later they all had their backs to the fixture, but when they turned they saw that it had started swinging again. They thought that perhaps someone walking on the floor above them could have caused a vibration that set it in motion, but they realized that they were the only ones in the house.

Kitchen Visitor and Eerie Sounds

Another incident involving the kitchen occurred one day when a staff member was outside. She looked through the kitchen window and saw a figure—she thought it must be a coworker—and waved to her. The person did not acknowledge the greeting and turned away. When the woman came into the house, she was surprised that no one was in the kitchen. She later found out that no one had been in the kitchen that day.

Footsteps and doors slamming have often be heard when no one else is in the house.

Recommendation

The outside of the house and the grounds are beautiful, but you should take the tour to really appreciate the stories of the people who lived here through the centuries, and see and the architecture, furniture, paintings, and personal items. (And of course, you don't want to miss that rocking horse or the staircase.) An orientation film on the history of the place is shown before the tours, and the staff members are very knowledgeable. There is also a gift shop selling books and videos.

About a dozen programs are held each year on Sundays from April to October.

Visitor Information

Gomez Mill House
11 Mill House Road
Marlboro, New York 12542
Phone/Fax: (845) 236-3126
gomezmillhouse@juno.com
www.gomez.org

Summer hours of operation: Wednesday to Sunday, 10 am to 4 pm. Tours begin at 10 am, 11:30 am, 1 pm, and 2:30 pm. Admission: $7.50 adults, $5 seniors, $2 students.

Directions

As listed on their Web site: Gomez Mill House is located on Mill House Road in the town of Marlboro, New York. Mill House is 5.2 miles north of the junction of Route 9W and I-84 (Newburgh Beacon Bridge) and ten miles south of the junction of Routes 44/55 (Poughkeepsie Bridge). Gomez Mill House is on the West Side of the Hudson River.

***If you arrive by bus it is very important that you DO NOT drive down Mill House Road. You must drop visitors off at the top of the hill (on 9W) and let them walk down fifty yards to the Mill House.

From Manhattan: Take the George Washington Bridge, to New Jersey upper level. Stay to your right and follow signs to take the Palisades Parkway north. Go through the Bear Mountain circle and follow signs for Route 9W North. Proceed approximately 25 miles through Newburgh. Note the intersection of I-84 and Route 9W (Lexus Diner will be on your left).

****Continue north on 9W, 5.2 miles. Slow down as you pass the Mill Creek Golf course. Mill House Road is the road on your right. The Gomez Mill House is the first House on your left. There is a small parking lot behind the house.

Tappan Zee Bridge west turns into I-87 NYS Thruway. Proceed North about 30 miles. Take Exit 17 Newburgh. Follow signs to I-84 EAST. Take exit 10. Go down the ramp and make a left at the light. Proceed as above**

Taconic Parkway north to exit marked Newburgh West/I-84 to Newburgh. Cross over the Newburgh Beacon Bridge (toll is \$ 1). Get off at exit 10; proceed down ramp onto Route 9W north. Proceed as above**

The Bottom Line

The History: The Gomez Mill House is the oldest Jewish residence in America, and has had almost three centuries of interesting inhabitants, including a Revolutionary War soldier and an artist. The film and tour are worth your time, and the special events offer a wide range of subjects from Dutch and Jewish history, to archaeology for children, to various subjects of local interest.

The Haunting: A mischievous boy with a Dutch boy haircut has been seen on the staircase, Emily Armstrong's rocking horse moves on its own, firemen responding to a fire refuse to return due to a mysterious incident, the light fixture in the kitchen moves, various figures have been seen, and voices, footsteps, and slamming doors have been heard. Staff has stated that not a season goes by without visitors with no prior knowledge of the place reporting strange encounters.

The Hasbrouck House at Washington's Headquarters
State Historic Site in Newburgh.

Washington's Headquarters

M any sites claim that "George Washington Slept Here," but how many places have the privilege of saying that Washington slept there for over a year, while making some of the most important and memorable decisions of his life?

Washington's Headquarters State Historic Site in Newburgh is one of those unique treasures that should be at the top of every history buff's list of places to visit. An entire book could be written about the period Washington stayed here, from April 1782 to August 1783, and the following will highlight some of the major events.

The original house was constructed in 1750 by Jonathan Hasbrouck, and you can see his mark "HB AD 1750" scratched into a stone above the door. He and his wife, Tryntje, had seven children, and the family became wealthy from their mill and other business pursuits. The house had two large additions by 1770, and when Washington made it his headquarters in 1782, a separate kitchen building was added, which no longer exists.

After Cornwallis surrendered at Yorktown in October of 1781, peace negotiations began. Although everyone expected a treaty to be signed, during the lengthy process Washington wanted to keep an eye on the British who still occupied New York City. He chose Newburgh as it was close enough that he could quickly be alerted if the redcoats were up to something, and it was far enough away that the fortifications at West Point and the chain across the Hudson would offer protection.

Washington leased the house from the Hasbroucks, and he and his staff took up residence in April of 1782. His wife, Martha, also joined him for much of his stay. (A beautiful watch that she owned is currently on display in the museum.) While the general and his top aides had bedrooms, other staff members slept in hallways. One can only imagine the hustle and bustle of officers coming and going, and the prolonged excitement and anticipation of waiting for news of final victory.

While many important decisions were made in the Hasbrouck house, four particularly notable events are worth special mention:

King George Washington?

In May of 1782, Colonel Lewis Nicola wrote to Washington in Newburgh complaining that Congress was inept, and not fit to run the new nation. Instead of this incompetent body of lawmakers, Nicola suggested that another monarchy should be established and that

Washington should become King of the United States. However, rather than embracing the idea of wearing a crown, Washington wrote to Nicola saying that he read the suggestion "with a mixture of great surprise and astonishment…no occurrence in the course of the War, has given me more painful sensations than your information of there being such ideas existing in the Army as you have expressed, and I must view with abhorrence, and reprehend with severity…You could not have found a person to whom your schemes are more disagreeable." Few men in history would have so vehemently refused the opportunity of becoming a king. It can be argued that of all of Washington's accomplishments and deeds, this was his greatest.

The Newburgh Conspiracy

In March of 1783, many officers had enough of Congress' empty promises of settling back pay and granting pensions. Tensions rose to the point where they openly spoke of marching an armed force to Congress and essentially staging a coup until their demands were met. Not only would this endanger the future of the fledging democracy, but if the British caught wind of a potential mutiny, they might be emboldened to resume hostilities. In response, Washington wrote a speech at the Hasbrouck house, which he then delivered to his officers at the nearby New Windsor Cantonment. The officers appeared unmoved until Washington hesitated to read a letter, and slowly fumbled for his glasses, which few had ever seen him wear. He then said, "Gentlemen, you will permit me to put on my spectacles, for I have not only grown gray but almost blind in the service of my country." With that one gesture the potential rebellion died, as the officers realized and appreciated the tremendous sacrifices their commanding general had made.

The Badge of Military Merit

Washington wanted to create something that would acknowledge "unusual gallantry, extraordinary fidelity and essential service," for privates and non-commissioned officers. On August 7, 1782, it was announced at his headquarters at the Hasbrouck house

The Tower of Victory.

that gallant soldiers would be awarded the Badge of Military Merit, which would be heart-shaped and made of purple cloth. This became the inspiration for President Herbert Hoover to create the Purple Heart medal, which was announced on Washington's 200th birthday on February 22, 1932.

"Cessation of Hostilities"

On April 19, 1783, exactly 8 years from the start of the war, Washington officially announced his order for the "cessation of hostilities," finally ending the long struggle for independence.

Washington also wrote about many important ideas during his stay here, such as his belief that there should be a strong federal government, shifting power away from the individual states. His thoughts and correspondence would be widely circulated and helped mold the form of government we have today.

The Hasbrouck property was acquired by the state in 1850 and became the first publicly operated historic site in the country. In the 1880s, a large monument, the "Tower of Victory," was built to commemorate the historic announcement Washington made at the Hasbrouck house, finally proclaiming the long war to be at an end. A museum was opened in 1910 and "The Minuteman" statue was added in 1924.

Countless school groups and tourists have visited Washington's Headquarters, so it is inevitable that, in all that time and with all those people, some rumors of ghosts would surface. While many who claim to be sensitive have reported feeling spirits—all good spirits, by the way—in the house and on the property, only one reliable source has had any encounter of note.

A former manager was alone in the Hasbrouck house one day when he saw a very tall woman with long black hair, wearing eighteenth century-style clothing, standing on the main staircase. In fact, Tryntje Hasbrouck was a tall woman with long black hair.

Back in 1782, it was reported that when told she would have to leave her home because Washington and his officers were moving in, Mrs. Hasbrouck handled the news in "sullen silence." Perhaps as a result of this episode, she still feels the need to keep an eye on whoever comes and goes from *her* home.

There have also been some odd noises in both the house and museum, particularly of footsteps and doors opening and closing. But as they are both old buildings, and with so many staff members and visitors constantly about, it's hard to say what can be categorized as unusual. Suffice to say that anything of the past that lingers here is just as friendly and curious as the visitors!

The original logs and links of chain which once spanned the
Hudson to block the British from sailing north.

Recommendation

If you have the slightest interest in George Washington, the Revolutionary War, or how people lived in the 1700s, this is unquestionably a "must see." The house is deceptively large and set up to look exactly like it would have been during Washington's stay. They even have a desk he actually used.

Other things of note: The enormous jambless Dutch fireplaces, the pane of glass where a new bride had scratched her name with her wedding ring, and of course the main staircase where Mrs. Hasbrouck keeps an eye on you.

The museum is small, but filled with fascinating one-of-a kind items. For example: two massive logs which were part of a barricade across the Hudson (the only two that have ever been retrieved from the Hudson), and a threatening-looking piece of a Cheveaux de Frise, which is essentially a pointed, iron-tipped defensive weapon that was placed on the bottom of the river to prevent British ships from sailing farther north (also the only one ever recovered).

There's also a wonderful model of the Hasbrouck house from the 1800s that has provided valuable information on both the interior and exterior. There's Martha Washington's watch, various household and military items, paintings, and numerous other artifacts.

There is an informative film that will help to understand the war and the role of the Hudson River.

On the grounds are the Minuteman statue, and the suitably massive and impressive Tower of Victory, all made more impressive by the beautiful views of the river. There is also the grave of Uzal Knapp, 1759-1856, one of the oldest surviving veterans of the war and one of Washington's personal guards (although there is some controversy on that point).

Visitor Information

Washington's Headquarters State Historic Site
84 Liberty Street
Newburgh, New York 12550
(845) 562-1195

Hours of Operation: April to October, Monday, and Wednesday thru Saturday, 10 am to 5 pm, Sunday 1-5pm. November to March: Open by appointment only. School and other groups welcome, special programs held monthly.

Special Events

Programs are held throughout the year, so call to get the latest schedule. Annual events include:

—Washington's Birthday celebration held Saturday-Monday every President's Weekend. Revolutionary War reenactor groups give demonstrations and there are special programs for the entire family throughout the weekend.

—Women's History Month presentation held one Sunday in March.

—Kites over the Hudson held the last Saturday in August. Free kites are given to the first 150 children, 15 and under. Prizes and refreshments.

—Winter with the Washingtons: Special opening 3 pm to 6 pm to coincide with Newburgh's Candlelight Tour during the Christmas season. The Hasbrouck House is decorated, there is live music, and hot cider and cookies.

Admission

$4 adults; $3 seniors and students; Free for children under 12.

Directions

As listed in their Web site: http://nysparks.com/sites/info.asp?siteID=32

From NYS Thruway: Exit 17, follow Route 17K east (Broadway) for 2 ¾ miles and make a right on Liberty Street. Take 3rd left onto LaFayette Street for parking

From 9W North: Turn left onto Broadway (Heading toward the Hudson River), turn right at Liberty Street. Take 3rd left onto LaFayette Street for parking.

From 9W South: Turn right onto Broadway (Heading toward the Hudson River), turn right at Liberty Street. Take 3rd left onto LaFayette Street for parking.

From I-84: Exit 10S, follow 9W south, turn left onto Broadway (Heading toward the Hudson River), turn right at Liberty Street. Take 3rd left onto LaFayette Street for parking.

The Bottom Line

The History: When you consider that some sites claim to be historic just because Washington spent a few hours napping there, Washington's Headquarters in Newburgh is head and shoulders above just about every other historic site in the Hudson Valley. So many events were initiated from this location that were of critical importance to the birth and infancy of this country—the refusal of a monarchy, the Newburgh conspiracy, the announcement of the end of the war, and the ideas about the formation of the government, etc.

The house gives you a wonderful sense of how it looked when Washington was there. The museum has artifacts you can't see elsewhere, and the grounds and view are beautiful.

The Haunting: Mrs. Hasbrouck appears to still be keeping a watchful eye on her house. Sounds and sensations have been experienced in the house, museum, and grounds.

The Ellison House in Vails Gate was used as a headquarters by General Henry Knox.

Knox's Headquarters

Like so many other private homes in so many other wars, the house of John Ellison in Vail's Gate was used as a military headquarters during the Revolutionary War. It was an ideal location, situated only two miles from the New Windsor Cantonment where 7,000 soldiers were encamped, and it was an elegant structure, suitable for gentleman officers. Generals Horatio Gates and Nathanael Greene both spent time here, but it is for the Chief of Artillery, General Henry Knox, for whom the site is named.

In 1741, the Ellisons began operating a lucrative grist mill on the Silver Stream. The labor was done by the several slaves they owned. The Ellison's Georgian-style stone home was built in 1754, and the family continued to prosper in milling and other businesses. Naturally, their lifestyle changed when the Continental Army came to town.

General Knox was something of a larger-than-life character, not the least of which was due to his sheer size, at over six feet tall and an estimated 300 pounds. His wife, Lucy, was also a very big woman, and at one point they were described as "the largest couple" in New York. Because of this, they had a special heavy-duty bed they traveled with, and used at the Ellison house.

Knox's early life in Boston was one of poverty, but he became a bookseller, who fortunately read extensively on military tactics. Among his later military accomplishments is his remarkable 300-mile journey from Fort Ticonderoga to Boston, transporting fifty-nine pieces of artillery in the dead of winter. As a result of this feat, the British were forced to abandon Boston in the face of so much firepower. After the war, Knox went on the serve as Secretary of War, and was one of the founders of the Society of the Cincinnati. He used the Ellison house as his headquarters from October 1782 until the spring of 1783.

For all the military activity that transpired here, does anything of that time still echo down the halls of the Ellison house? There is a story about the young Kitty Wint, who fell in love with one of the soldiers. They decided to run away together and planned to meet at the end of a tunnel which went from the Ellison house to the Silver Stream. Unfortunately, the soldier died before the scheduled rendezvous. Forever heartbroken by the loss of her love, even after death, Kitty's ghost was said to continue to walk the house and grounds searching for her soldier.

It is almost impossible to say how stories such as this began, or how they evolve over the generations. Could there be some basis in fact for the girl who lost her love? Possibly, but there never was a tunnel leading from the house to the stream. There was a relative of the Ellisons named

Gitty Wynkoop who signed her name in one of the window panes in the house—could Kitty Wint be a corruption of that name? Certainly many young women lost soldiers during the war, and perhaps elements of the story were simply changed over the years.

One tale which is most assuredly completely fanciful is that of the "Witch's Stairs." There is a unique set of stairs in the Ellison house leading to a storage attic. The stairs are narrow and triangular, so that the user must alternate one foot at a time on the thicker part of each stair. (It could not have been the easiest way of carrying goods up to the attic.) At some point, a story was created that a witch chased anyone who attempted to go up into that attic. Fortunately, as witches apparently have very large feet, she was unable to climb the unusual stairs and always tripped and fell, and so never caught anyone. Why she just didn't simply wait for her victim to come back down the stairs is not explained, but that would have ruined a perfectly good fairy tale.

Recommendation

The house is beautiful and appears as it would have been during the time of the Ellisons, so you will get an excellent taste of what life was like in the area over 200 years ago. Check out the slave quarters and ruins of the grist mill, and of course, take a look at the Witch's Stairs. The Jane Colden Native Plant Sanctuary (Jane was America's first woman botanist) is also on the grounds, and there are wooded trails for hiking or cross-county skiing.

To get the full Revolutionary War experience, also visit the New Windsor Cantonment, just two miles away.

Visitor Information

Knox's Headquarters State Historic Site
Forge Hill Road
Vails Gate, New York 12584
(845) 561-5498
http://nysparks.state.ny.us/sites/info.asp?siteId=18

Seasons/Hours: Memorial Day thru Labor Day, Wednesday to Saturday, 10 am to 5 pm; Sunday, 1 to 5 pm. Other times by appointment only. Admission: $3 adults, $2 NYS senior citizens, free for children 12 and under. Group tours must be scheduled in advance. Call for information on the latest calendar of events.

Directions

From their Web site:

From I-84: Exit 7-S take Route 300 South for 3.5 miles to railroad track, turn left after track. Proceed straight through traffic light to stop sign, turn left onto Route 94. At next traffic light, turn right onto Forge Hill Road. Knox's Headquarters is on your right.

From I-87 (NYS Thruway): Exit 17 for Newburgh, turn right onto Route 17K for 0.75 mile, then left onto Route 300 and follow above directions.

From Route 9W: Turn at traffic light onto Forge Hill Road. Proceed for 1.5 miles, Knox's Headquarters is on the left.

The Bottom Line

The History: A fine example of a Hudson Valley home from 1754 that was used by General Henry Knox and other officers as a headquarters during the Revolutionary War.

The Haunting: The story of a young woman forever searching for her lost love.

Section 4

The "Witch's Stairs." *Courtesy of Knox's Headquarters State Historic Site.*

One of the cannons at Fort Montgomery State Historic Site, pointing south down the Hudson River. The narrow bend in the river and the steep hills made this an ideal location for a fort.

Fort Montgomery

The year 1777 looked to be a dark time for the cause of American liberty. The prior year, 1776, had ended with New York City falling into the hands of the British. In February of 1777, British General Howe hoped to be warm and comfortable in Philadelphia by the time the next winter set in again. As painful as the loss of these two cities would be, however, the real *coup de grâce* was to be seizing control of the Hudson River. The British saw the river as the key to cutting the lines of communication and supplies between the northern and southern halves of the rebellious colonies. They believed that if this campaign was successful, the war would come to a swift end.

The plan called for the bold and overconfident General John Burgoyne to move south from Canada. Colonel Barry St. Leger was to move from the west through the Mohawk Valley, and General Sir Henry Clinton and his forces would come north from New York City. These armies would sweep away all the rebels in their paths and they would have a glorious victory celebration when they all met in Albany, New York.

It was a great plan on paper, but then, the American patriots developed a knack for spoiling British parties.

One of the first pieces of the British victory puzzle to be lost was when General Howe decided that he and his 10,000 men would concentrate on taking Philadelphia instead of marching to New York. St. Leger became entangled in a long and unsuccessful siege of Fort Stanwix and had to turn back. General Clinton was slow to begin his campaign, and then ran into some stubborn resistance at a couple of forts on the west side of the Hudson River in October of 1777.

Realizing the vital importance of the river, in 1775 Congress had authorized the construction of fortifications along its banks. One site that was chosen was where the Popolopen Creek entered the river at a narrow point of the Hudson that was only about 500 yards wide. A heavy iron chain was placed across the river here to prevent British ships sailing any farther north. A point of land overlooking the chain on the north side of the creek made an excellent location for a battery of cannons to add another line of river defense, and thus it was the local geography that dictated the location of Fort Montgomery. Fort Clinton was constructed on the south side of the creek, and a pontoon bridge connected the two fortifications.

In early October when General Clinton sailed up the river with about 3,100 troops, he tried to make it look as though he was landing his soldiers on the east side of the river. However, the following morning under the cover of fog, the British forces—consisting of Hessian mercenaries, local Loyalists, and British regulars—came ashore at Stony Point and made their way toward the two forts.

The British began assaulting the forts from the west on land, and from ships in the river below late in afternoon of the 6th of October. They greatly outnumbered the American forces, and of those 600-700 defenders, only half of them were army regulars, the rest being local militia. Despite the uneven numbers, the fortifications and artillery initially helped hold back the British, but by evening it was obvious that it would only be a matter of time.

To prevent "further effusion of blood," British Lieutenant Colonel Mungo Campbell approached Fort Montgomery with a flag of truce and offered the Americans terms—if they surrendered immediately, they would all receive good treatment. The American officer, Colonel William Livingston, is said to have boldly replied to Campbell that if the British surrendered immediately, they would also be treated well.

Apparently, Campbell was not amused by the American sense of humor, and the attack was renewed. Unfortunately for Campbell, he was to discover just how determined the Americans were to fight on, as he was killed leading his men against one of the redoubts of Fort Montgomery. Fighting was fierce, and acts of bravery were recorded on both sides, although perhaps none can compare with that of American Lieutenant Timothy Mix.

As the British began to overrun Fort Montgomery, he prepared to fire his cannon. At that moment, a shot blew off his right hand. Without hesitating, he grabbed a match with his left hand and fired the cannon right into a group of about forty British troops, with deadly effect. (Remarkably, Timothy Mix survived, and lived until 1824.)

As night fell, the British gained entry into both forts and overwhelmed the defenders with their superior numbers in brutal hand-to-hand combat. At Fort Montgomery, the majority of this fighting occurred in the areas of the Round Hill and North Redoubts. An interesting and poignant fact to consider here is that this section of the fort was being attacked by New York Loyalists, so it was actually New Yorkers fighting New Yorkers.

Under the cover of darkness, some of the Americans were able to escape, but of the regulars and militia at the two forts, an estimated 350 were killed, wounded or captured—a staggering fifty percent casualty rate. And despite the promises of fair treatment, the prisoners were sent to the infamous Sugar House in New York City, and to floating prisons known as "hell ships" where many died of starvation and disease.

The British suffered about 190 casualties, but the Battle of Fort Clinton and Fort Montgomery was a satisfying victory for them. They occupied the forts until word came to retreat back to New York City, then they set fire to all the structures, exploded the powder magazines, and reduced both forts to rubble. They also severed the chain across the river.

However, ultimately the British campaign in New York would be a failure, as reinforcements never reached Burgoyne, who was compelled to surrender at Saratoga on October 17. It was a critical victory that helped convince France to join the patriot cause in 1778, and the rest as they say, is history.

While there were several firsthand accounts describing the events of the battle and some excellent histories have been written, there is still one very intriguing mystery—what happened to all of the bodies from Fort Montgomery? It has been a popular legend in the area that the fallen soldiers were thrown into Hessian Lake (to the south, by the present Bear Mountain Inn). As a result, for many years the lake was called Bloody Pond, with the name later changed to reflect the remains of the Hessian mercenaries that were allegedly concealed in its depths.

However, while that could be a possibility for the those killed at Fort Clinton, which is much closer, the very knowledgeable staff at Fort Montgomery points out that it is highly unlikely that the British would take the time and considerable effort to gather all of the bodies from Fort Montgomery, carry them across the creek and down to Hessian Lake.

What is more likely is that they would either leave the rebels where they fell, or toss them into the closest body of water. And according to the eyewitness account of an army chaplain named Dr. Dwight, who visited the sites of the forts a few months after the battle, that's exactly what was done. The following account is both sad and provocative, in the sense that there are most likely the remains of many brave soldiers somewhere beneath the feet of all the tourists who walk the battlefield today.

Dr. Dwight wrote:

"I went down the river in company with several officers, to examine the forts Clinton and Montgomery, built on a point six or eight miles below West Point, for the defense of the river. The first object which met our eyes, after we left our barge and ascended the bank, was the remains of a fire kindled by the cottagers of this solitude, for the purpose of consuming the bones of some of the Americans who

The stone foundation of soldiers' barracks.

Stone foundations from the fort's structures.
Route 9W runs through the grounds of the fort
which covers over fourteen acres.

had fallen at this place, and had been left unburied. Some of these bones were lying partially consumed round the spot where the fire had been kindled; and some had evidently been converted into ashes.

"As we went onward, we were distressed by the fetor of decayed human bodies. To me this was a novelty; and more overwhelming and dispiriting than I am able to describe. As we were attempting to discover the source from which it proceeded, we found, at a small distance from Fort Montgomery, a pond of a moderate size, in which we saw the bodies of several men, who had been killed in the assault upon the fort. They were thrown into this pond, the preceding autumn, by the British, when probably the water was sufficiently deep to cover them. Some of them were covered at this time; but a depth so small, as to leave them distinctly visible. Others had an arm, a leg, and a part of the body above the surface. The clothes which they wore when they were killed, were still on them; and proved that they were militia; being the ordinary dress of farmers. Their faces were bloated and monstrous; and their postures were uncouth, distorted, and in the highest degree afflictive.

"My companions had been accustomed to the horrors of war, and sustained the prospect with some degree of firmness. To me, a novice in scenes of this nature, it was overwhelming. I surveyed it for a moment and hastened away. From this combination of painful objects we proceeded to Fort Clinton, built on a rising ground, at a small distance further down the river. The ruins of this fortress were a mere counterpart of those of Fort Montgomery. Every combustible in both had been burnt; and what was not, was extensively thrown down. Every thing which remained was a melancholy picture of destruction."

Several things become apparent from this account. First, the British had little regard for their enemy—particularly the local militia—and made no efforts to giving these men a proper burial. Also, the "pond of a moderate size" a "small distance from Fort Montgomery" where the bodies of the militia were dumped cannot possibly be Hessian Lake, as that lake, as was pointed out earlier, is on the other side of the Popolopen Creek to the south, nearer Fort Clinton. When Dr. Dwight looked upon these figures sticking out of the shallow water, he was very close to the remains of Fort Montgomery, and had yet to go "further down the river" to Fort Clinton.

So where, then, was this small, nearby body of water? A former manager of the site thoroughly researched the history of the battle, and then carefully walked the grounds of the fort and the immediate surrounding area, and found a few potential locations along the northern stretch of the grounds that could have contained ponds that would vary in depth depending upon the season.

Without digging, however, it's all speculation. While the actual location isn't certain, one thing is for sure—the remains of these gallant patriots are still there, and perhaps it is their spirits that are still glimpsed today.

For example, one night, people were arriving at the visitor's center at Fort Montgomery to attend a lecture. One man came in and started to compliment the staff on the authentic-looking reenactor they had hired. As there were no reenactors as part of the program, they asked the man what he had seen.

He explained that as he was pulling into the parking lot, he clearly saw "a man dressed in an old hunting frock" standing close by on the grounds of the fort. He looked real and solid and just as if he had stepped out of the 1700s. No one else had seen the man, who appeared to be dressed in the manner of American militia, and upon further investigation was nowhere to be found.

The Fort Montgomery Visitor's Center and the Bear Mountain Bridge.

Another remarkable sighting occurred just a short distance to the north of the fort in a small office building built on what would have been the grounds of the original battlefield. One day, an employee witnessed the distinct figure of a British soldier as he walked through the lobby and then disappeared into a wall. Obviously, this wasn't a reenactor, either.

Another fascinating aspect of the history of this site is the fact that long before the first stone of the fort was put in place, Native Americans lived on this land. Inside the walls of Fort Montgomery is one very large rock that Native Americans had once used for shelter (there are two such rocks on the property), as was evidenced by the many artifacts that were unearthed beneath it. Other signs of old Indian campgrounds have been found by the Grand Battery, and most recently, an arrowhead was uncovered while digging for the foundation of the visitor's center. The presence of these ancient residents has been felt on the grounds of the fort and in the visitor's center, and there have been numerous inexplicable sights and sounds.

In fact, quite a few things have gone bump in the night (and during the day) at this new center. Footsteps, voices, and figures have often been witnessed. It's never anything threatening, but it certainly gives one the sense that history is literally still alive at Fort Montgomery, in more ways than one!

Recommendation

Fort Montgomery spreads over fourteen acres containing sections of the original fortifications, the foundations of soldier barracks and other buildings, and Indian rock shelters. To fully appreciate the scope of the battle and the brave acts of the soldiers who fought here, you must walk the grounds. If you have the stamina, you can also go down the hill and cross the footbridge over to Fort Clinton, or you can drive over to that site. Maps of the sites are available at the visitor's center.

The visitor center at Fort Montgomery is a little architectural gem that has spectacular views of the Hudson River from its glass-walled exhibit room. There are many authentic battlefield artifacts on display. The theater shows an excellent fourteen-minute orientation film, and there's a large three-dimensional map that really helps in understanding the layout of the forts. The staff is very knowledgeable and helpful, and they can answer any questions you might have about the British and American forces involved in the battle, and exactly how the events played out.

Seeing the actual items belonging to the soldiers who fought and died here really adds a personal connection to this important place and time in history. Don't forget to look closely at the cuff buttons in the special display case by the theater. Featured in the film, the buttons are enameled with the word "Liberty" and speak both to the dedication of the American soldier who wore them, and the tragedy of why they were left behind, only to be discovered almost two centuries later during an archaeological dig of the grounds.

Visitor Information

Fort Montgomery State Historic Site
Route 9W
Fort Montgomery, New York 10922
(845) 446-2134
http://nysparks.state.ny.us/sites/info.asp?siteId=36

Visitor's Center hours are 9 am to 5 pm, Wednesday through Sunday.

Rates for Visitor's Center and grounds: $3 per adult, $2 per senior/student, children 12 and under free. Parking is free.

Fort Montgomery grounds are open 7 days a week, sunrise to sunset.

Attractions include audio-visual programs, demonstrations, group tours, hiking, interpretive signs, scenic views, and self-guided tours.

Directions

From the East-Route 202, 6, or 9D to the Bear Mountain Bridge: In the traffic circle take your first right to 9W North. The entrance to Fort Montgomery will be on your right just after you cross the bridge.

From New York City: Take the Palisades Parkway north to the Bear Mountain Circle or take the New York State Thruway to exit 16 in Harriman, then Route 6 toward Bear Mountain. At the circle the third right will be 9W North. The entrance to Fort Montgomery will be on your right just after you cross the bridge.

The Bottom Line

The History: Fort Montgomery is an important Revolutionary War site that is more intact than most other contemporary battlefields. The visitor center staff and displays are very informative, and a guided tour is really worth your time.

The Haunting: Revolutionary War-era soldiers have been seen on the grounds. The presence of Native Americans has been felt. Many strange occurrences have been experienced in the visitor's center.

In the early 1700s, Caldwell's Landing, now Jones' Point in Tomkins Cove, was a regular stop for sailors on their journeys up and down the Hudson River, as there was a popular tavern there.

There is a story that near this tavern, in the early summer of 1720, a Spanish ship dropped anchor. Dark-haired men with scowling faces left the ship carrying picks and shovels and headed into the woods. Months passed before these men were seen again, and when they finally returned, they were carrying large, heavy sacks. One of these men brought his sack into the tavern and as the liquor began to loosen the stranger's tongue, he began to talk about what he and his comrades had been doing all summer. He then revealed the contents of his burden to one of the locals. The sack was filled with silver ore!

The moment the Spaniards sailed away, some of the local men went into the woods in an attempt to discover the silver mine, but found nothing but a crude cabin on Black Mountain. A year or two later, the Spaniards returned with empty sacks and their picks and shovels. Again, after several months, they returned laden with valuable silver ore. This continued for several more years, yet still, the frustrated residents could not find the source of the treasure.

Silver Mine

Looking across the lake to Black Mountain where legend says there is a lost Spanish silver mine.

Then one year, six Spaniards went into the woods, but this time only two of the men returned and immediately got on their ship and sailed away. Two locals hurried to the cabin on Black Mountain, and discovered an awful site. Instead of treasure, they found the bodies of two murdered men on the floor. One had had his skull broken, while the other had a Spanish dagger buried deep in his chest.

After they overcame the initial shock, they realized that two other Spaniards were still missing. Although darkness was falling, they headed toward the summit of the mountain in search of the missing men. (Of course, if they happened to find the opening to the mine, that would be even better.) However, what they found, or what found them, was even more terrifying than the bloody scene in the cabin.

As the last rays of sunlight fell beneath the horizon, strange lights appeared. The men froze as the lights rushed toward them and they could see that it was actually the eerily glowing forms of the missing Spaniards. The men tried to run, but were frozen in place all night. Finally, when the first light of dawn touched the top of Black Mountain, the ghosts suddenly vanished and the men were able to move.

Over the years people laughed about the stories of Spanish ghosts, but many local residents had frightening experiences on that mountain. The Spaniards' cabin long ago decayed to nothingness, but the legend lives on. To this day, visitors to Silver Mine park occasionally cannot resist the lure of lost treasure, and they hike back to Black Mountain hoping to find the opening to the mine which cost the lives of at least four men. Geologists do admit that silver could exist in these mountains, but so far no one has uncovered any large deposits.

SILVER MINE
PICNIC AREA
←

Section 4

Recommendation

Driving through Harriman State Park affords beautiful views of the woods and lakes any season of the year. If you are up to some exercise, put on your hiking boots and take a walk around the Silver Mine Lake. The missing mine is allegedly on the north side of the lake on Black Mountain.

In recent years, authorities were alerted to strange noises coming from Black Mountain. Park rangers and police went to investigate and they apprehended a couple of over-eager treasure hunters who believed the legends of Spanish silver and were using dynamite to try to locate the old mine! (A friendly warning—this is not only dangerous, but quite illegal, and anyone attempting such a stunt will be arrested. Handling dynamite is also a good way to turn yourself into a ghost.)

Visitor Information

The Silver Mine area of Harriman State Park is open year round and offers picnic grounds, fishing, boat launch sites, and hiking. Fishing and boating permits required. Dogs must be kept on a leash.

Directions

As listed in their Web site at www.nysparks.state.ny.us/parks/info.asp?parkID=158

Palisades Interstate Parkway to exit 18. In the traffic circle take Seven Lakes Drive to Silver Mine park (on your left).

The Bottom Line

The History: How much is history, how much is legend? There could be a silver mine in the area, and ships did regularly stop at Caldwell's Landing, so there could be truth to the tale.

The Haunting: Many people have reported experiencing an eerie feeling back in the woods. The story of glowing Spanish ghosts at sunset is at least worth the drive, if not a good hike.

Section Five

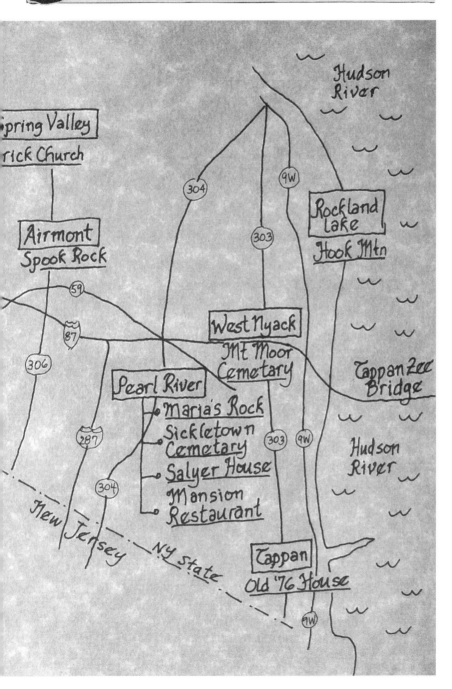

The Tappan Zee Bridge spans a section
of the Hudson River once thought to be
haunted by a ghost ship.

Directions

The bridge spans the Hudson River via Route 87/287/New York
State Thruway between South Nyack in Rockland and Tarrytown in
Westchester Counties.

Notes: Zee is the Dutch word for sea, the area was once inhabited
by the Tappan Indians, hence the name. The bridge opened in 1955
connecting Rockland and Westchester, opening the floodgates of development in Rockland County.

Shatemuc was an Algonquin term meaning "the water that flows
both ways," which the river does as it is technically a tidal estuary.

The beautiful river that the Indians called the Shatemuc underwent a name change thanks to an English explorer working for the Dutch. Henry Hudson first sailed up the river in 1609, and in recognition for his achievement this historic waterway now bears his name. One might envy Hudson for being commemorated in such a way, but before you get too green, consider his fate.

In 1610, Hudson made another voyage to the New World, this time entering the great bay in Canada that would also come to bear his name. After enduring a brutal winter along the shores of the bay, Hudson's long-suffering crew had had enough. They mutinied and set their captain, his son, and seven other sailors adrift in a small boat. The abandoned men were never seen again.

The story of Hudson's tragic demise was a popular tale to tell amongst the Dutch colonists living in the area of what is now Westchester and Rockland Counties, and like most stories, it became embellished over the years. Thus the legend of the Ghost Ship of the Hudson was born. The majority of the alleged sightings on the river occurred in stormy weather (perhaps after a few drinks to stave off a chill?), in the general location of the present-day Tappan Zee Bridge. In addition to seeing the shadowy figure of an old Dutch ship, witnesses claimed to be able to hear the screams of the tormented crew in between claps of thunder.

Today, people still hear screaming near the bridge, only rather than coming from a ghost ship, it's from commuters stuck in the legendary traffic.

In the eighteenth century there was a Native American named Comboan living in the woods of Nyack, where Brookside and Clinton Avenues are today. He was a skilled tracker and hunter and knew every inch of land for miles around. The colonists liked and trusted Comboan, and often asked for his help, which he always graciously gave.

One night they asked for Comboan's help in a matter of life and death. Two small children had wandered away from the village and had become lost in the black depths of the forest. Even though they had been gone for three days and there had been heavy rains that would have washed away their footprints, Comboan immediately put his years of tracking experience to work and found the children. They were cold, exhausted, and half-starved, but they were alive.

There was a great celebration, with everyone thanking the old tracker for saving the lives of the missing children. Thinking they were offering a wonderful gift, the parents of the children offered to have Comboan baptized into the Christian religion. Comboan's people had always worshipped the Great Spirit that they believed resided in the area below Hook Mountain, and he politely declined. He was a man of the woods and his faith was in the spirits who dwelt there.

While Comboan kept his faith, the residents of Nyack cruelly broke theirs. With the onset of the French and Indian War in the 1750s, people began to become suspicious of any Native American. Their imaginations ran wild, and they came up with the implausible story that Comboan was planning to slaughter them all in their sleep. The people of Nyack went so far as to put Comboan on trial for his alleged plot. He, of course, declared his innocence. The people were not convinced. He talked of the many times he was asked to help the settlers, and of how he had saved the lives of two of their children. The people were unmoved. Comboan was sentenced to a fate worse than death—banishment from his beloved Nyack, forced to leave the land of his ancestors and the Great Spirit.

Soon after the old man was driven from his home and out of the county, it was reported that he had died, perhaps of a broken heart. Many years later, however, people smelled burning wood and saw wisps of a campfire smoke coming from the area where Comboan used to hunt. No fires could be found, but they did find hunting traps that no

Hook Mountain

Does Comboan's ghost still pray here to the Great Spirit beneath Hook Mountain?

A nearby street pays tribute to the Native American who once called this land home, before being unjustly exiled.

one but Comboan could have devised. They also began to see moccasin prints where no one had walked.

Perhaps it was their collective guilt that made them experience these things, or perhaps Comboan's spirit had returned to the land he loved. For years, people were too afraid to walk in the fields and down the paths by Hook Mountain where Comboan had lived, giving the area the name Spook Hollow. As time passed, however, the legend of the old man faded from memory and progress brought developments to the once-wild forests of Nyack. Yet even in this century, there have been strange things going on at the base of that mountain. Several people, unaware of the stories of the past, spoke of seeing an old Indian offering prayers skyward. Others told of soft footsteps following them, almost as if the person was wearing moccasins, but no one could be seen.

Today, with all the picnickers, hikers, and cyclists filling the park at Hook Mountain, and jet skiers buzzing up and down the river, it's hard to imagine a time when the area was peaceful and unspoiled. If you do happen to find a quiet evening to take a walk beneath the rugged mountains, pause for a moment and try to picture the land as Comboan knew it. In those last amber rays of sunlight, you might also want to check the ground for moccasin prints, sniff the air for smoke, and as you walk back to your car, remember that you might not be alone.

Recommendation

Hook Mountain is beautiful in all seasons, but it can get very crowded on weekends in summer. There is an excellent path right along the river which is a great place for a walk or bicycle ride, or pack a picnic lunch and just to sit and take in the views.

Visitor Information

Hook Mountain is located in Nyack Beach State Park
698 N. Broadway
Upper Nyack, New York 10960
Phone: (845) 268-3020
http://nysparks.state.ny.us/parks/info.asp?parkID=62

Open year round for day use.

Directions

From the west on New York State Thruway, take exit 11 and turn right towards US-9W / Nyack/South Nyack. Turn left (east) onto Route 59. Turn left (north) onto US-9W (N. Highland Avenue) Turn right (east) onto 6th Avenue. Turn left (north) onto North Broadway and proceed to park entrance.

From the Tappan Zee Bridge, take exit 11 on the New York State Thruway. Turn right onto ramp towards US-9W/Nyack. Stay straight onto High Avenue. Turn left (north) onto US-9W (North Highland Avenue). Turn right (east) onto 6th Avenue. Turn left (north) onto North Broadway and proceed to park entrance.

The Bottom Line

The History: An Indian named Comboan lived in this area in the 1700s. He was always helpful to the settlers, and was unjustly banished from his home.

The Haunting: An Indian is seen offering prayers toward the sky. Footsteps are heard and people feel as if they are being followed.

Established in 1776, the Sickletown Cemetery contains the remains of eighteen Revolutionary War soldiers.

There is an historic marker at the gate of the Sickletown Cemetery that commemorates the eighteen Revolutionary War veterans who are buried here. Perhaps they should also have a plaque to acknowledge the restless spirits.

Eyewitnesses have seen a misty figure across the street, which then floated over the road and passed right through the gates of the cemetery. While this particular spirit has not been identified, there is a clue as to the identity of another restless soul who has been spotted on the grounds of the cemetery, or above them, to be more accurate.

Several decades ago, a boy tied a rope to a tree in the cemetery, and used it to swing over a stream and jump in. One day his timing was off, and he fell to his death in the cemetery. Since then, local residents claim to still see the figure of the boy moving through the air above the graves.

Visitor Information

The cemetery gate is kept locked, but you can read some of the grave stones through the chain link fence, or you can simply wait for something ethereal to float by.

Sickletown Cemetery

A misty spirit has been seen floating across the street and entering the Sickletown Cemetery.

Directions

From the Palisades Parkway take Exit 7 and head east on East Townline Road. Turn right on Sickletown Road. The road will go back over the parkway and from that point the cemetery will be about 0.5 miles on the left, just before Briarwood Lane.

The Bottom Line

The History: The burial site of eighteen Revolutionary War soldiers.

The Haunting: A misty form floats across the street and through the gates, and the figure of a boy is seen above the cemetery.

The castle-like Mansion Restaurant at Blue Hill with its rolling green golf course was built in 1900 by Montgomery Maze as a private home. Its rough stone walls stand in sharp contrast to the interior's finely-carved mahogany woodwork and Tiffany stained glass. Anyone should have felt extremely fortunate to be able to call such a place home, but it was actually only used as a warm-weather "party house."

Over a hundred years later, the spirit of the place is basically the same, only now the parties are catered affairs at the Mansion's restaurant, and the stables no longer house horses, but golf carts. In a county of rampant over-development and bustling malls, a visit to this tranquil mansion on the hill above the lake, surrounded by a golf course with trees and lush grass, gives one the opportunity to take a deep breath and enjoy the beautiful vistas.

One can only imagine what the parties here were like in the elegant days of early 1900s, the rambunctious Roaring Twenties, or after the repeal of Prohibition. It may not have been all fun and games at this

Mansion Restaurant

The Mansion Restaurant was the built as a summer
party house in 1900 by Montgomery Maze.

house, however, as there is a story that a girl was found drowned in a pond the morning after a party. Was it an accident, or an unsolved murder? Also, the builder's grandson, Robert Montgomery Maze, may have died in the house from an illness while still a young man.

Perhaps these tragic events have left a lasting impression on the house, as for decades, restaurant staff have witnessed shadowy figures throughout the building. One patron even saw the distinct figure of a young man holding a book walk into a second floor room. Research revealed that the room had been a library when the house was first built, and it is suspected that the figure was that of Robert Montgomery Maze.

Much of the activity here is of the harmless but mischievous variety, with wall-mounted sconces being spun around, tablecloths turned over, and other benign but obvious signs that someone is trying to get noticed. There are also the sounds of footsteps heard when the place is locked and no one else is around. One employee was so convinced someone was in the building trying play a trick on him that he went back outside to check for additional footprints in the new snow, but found only his.

For many years, female guests reported that the ladies room on the second floor felt haunted, but perhaps recent renovations have broken that spell.

Visitor Information

Mansion Restaurant at Blue Hill Golf Club
285 Blue Hill Road
Pearl River, New York 10965
(845)735-4818

Directions

Palisades Parkway to Exit 6W (Orangeburg Road-Pearl River), then take a right at third traffic light (Blue Hill Road). The golf course entrance is 0.5 miles on the left side.

Please note: While the restaurant is usually open to the public, private parties are often held, so call ahead.

Recommendation

The Blue Hill Golf Club is a municipal course open to the public, so here is a rare chance to combine ghosts and golf! The mansion restaurant has a café and bar section open to the public. The best way to experience the main house is to attend one of the catered affairs, and it is a beautiful setting for weddings and special events.

The Bottom Line

The History: A replica of a castle built in 1900 as a summer party house, containing magnificent woodwork and a huge Tiffany window.

The Haunting: The spirit of a girl drowned during a party, the figure of a man carrying a book, many shadowy figures seen, footsteps, and mischievous activity.

Section 5

The sandstone Salyer House was built in the 1700s.

Salyer House

The exact year the Salyer House was built is not certain, but it was during the last quarter of the eighteenth century. It could have already been standing during the Revolution, as there is a story that there was a skirmish in the area, and one of the men was brought to the Salyer House, and subsequently died of his wounds. The story is not documented, however, so the best historians can say for certain is that the house was constructed in the late 1700s.

The original owners, Michael and Elizabeth Salyer, had four daughters, and thanks to the old Dutch system allowing women to inherit property (unlike the British laws), it was daughter Mary who inherited the house and 9.2 acres of land in 1810. Mary married David Bogert, and they sold the house in 1825 to James and Charity DeClark. Anyone familiar with local history—or street and town names in the area—will immediately recognize these early family names.

In 1966, the house began a somewhat less domestic chapter when it was purchased by the United Water Company. While it did house employees and their families, that traditional pride of ownership was gone, and the house was not so lovingly maintained. When United Water donated the house to the Town of Orangetown in 1992, it required four years of interior and exterior restoration by many dedicated volunteers. Their combined efforts brought about the opening of the Orangetown Historical Museum at the Salyer House in 1996.

Of special note to those interested in Hudson Valley and Revolutionary War history is their exhibit "A Spy in our Midst: Major John André," which looks at the famous British spy in the Benedict Arnold affair, and "Our Dutch Sandstone Houses" which examines Dutch architecture through photos of these early local dwellings.

Is there also something of interest here for those looking for a more unusual experience? Staff members have seen a man in late eighteenth-century civilian clothing standing in one of the front rooms on the first floor. Could it be Michael Salyer? Even those who haven't witnessed any figures do admit that "something is in this house," although no one is concerned, as it is definitely a benign spirit.

Whether or not Michael Salyer is the man keeping watch over his home, he must be pleased by how the place has been preserved. After all, what more could any of us ask for, to have something of our lives become part of history and provide our descendants a window into the past.

Recommendation

While you can drive by any time to see and photograph the house, do try to attend one of their special events and see the exhibits. The Orangetown Historical Museum and Archives includes the Dutch sandstone DePew House nearby at 196 Blaisdell Road, Orangeburg, and they also host special events and exhibits.

Visitor Information

The Salyer House
Orangetown Historical Museum & Archives
196 Blue Hill Road
Pearl River, New York 10965
(845) 398-1302

Open Sundays from 1 to 4 pm, school group or weekday tours by appointment.
Donations requested.

The Bottom Line

The History: A fine example of late 1700s Dutch sandstone architecture, owned by members of some of the area's earliest families.

The Haunting: A man in late 1700s clothing is seen, and a presence is felt.

By the time Casparus Mabie be-gan building his house on Main Street in 1753, Tappan was already an old town. The grant for a township had been issued in 1686; by 1691 there was a courthouse, and a church was built in 1694. Tappan was an important center in early colonial days, and Mabie's house would play an important role in the coming Revolution.

Patriots would meet at the house to discuss the latest news and share information, and it came to be known as the "listening post." George Washington and many of his generals dined at the house—events that were catered by Samuel Fraunces, of the famed Fraunces Tavern in Manhattan. Arguably, though, its most famous role would be as a jail, when British Major John André was held there for his trial and execution.

In September of 1780, Major André received the plans for West Point from the notorious American traitor, General Benedict Arnold. When the treasonous plot was uncovered, Arnold escaped to the safety of the British lines, but André was taken prisoner. He was brought to Tappan and held in Mabie's house.

The Old '76 House

The Old '76 House was a tavern for patriots, a prison for a spy, and is now a fine restaurant.

On September 29, Major André was put on trial at the church across the street. The recommendation that the board of inquiry delivered to George Washington stated that this British officer caught in civilian clothes "ought to be considered as a spy from the enemy" and "ought to suffer death" as a consequence. Washington signed the death warrant and André's fate was sealed.

On October 2, André was taken from the Mabie house and led to the place of his execution. Ever the gentleman and brave soldier, he put the noose around his own neck, and tied a handkerchief over his eyes. As he had predicted, there was only a "momentary pang" as death was almost immediate, and his body was buried on the spot where he died.

The famous house became a tavern in 1800, and for most of the next 200 years, the "1776 House" continued to serve the public, becoming one of the country's oldest such establishments. Today, the fully restored and expanded Old '76 House is a colonial gem, which is best appreciated while dining by one of its fireplaces, or perhaps gathering with family and friends for Sunday brunch. However, if it's more than just food and history you're looking for, you probably won't be disappointed—this 250-year-old house just might also have some of the country's oldest ghosts...

Major André (Of Course!)

Several people have seen a man in a British officer's uniform who fits the description of Major André.

Noisy Ghosts

There are eyewitness accounts dating back several decades indicating that something of the house's colorful history may still be echoing down its halls and stairways. There was a dishwasher named Baltimore who lived alone upstairs for many years. He would often hear footsteps and voices throughout the house and quickly came to realize that all of this activity did not come from the world of the living. Although terrified by the bold and noisy ghosts, they at least did not enter his room. However, just in case they ever did, Baltimore kept a rope ladder by his window so he could make a quick escape from the house!

Over the years, other employees have also heard footsteps and voices. On at least one occasion, the police were called because it sounded like someone was upstairs after the restaurant had closed, but no one was found. The early morning hours also seem to be popular with at least one ghost who has often been heard coming down the staircase from the second floor.

People walking by late at night after the place is closed and empty have reported loud sounds, as if furniture is being moved.

Table #2

If you want a prime paranormal seat, request Table #2. Tablecloths on that table have been seen to move on their own. There was a loud sound of silverware crashing to the floor by Table #2, but when the staff came to see what happened, not a thing was out of place. The most common occurrence at Table #2 involves the glass flue. All of the tables are set in colonial style, and each has a candleholder with a glass flue. There has never been any problem with these candleholders, except at Table #2. The glass flue is often found laying on the table or the floor. No one can figure out why the flue repeatedly comes off of its base, or why it hasn't broken when it falls to the floor. No one has actually seen or heard it happen, but just about everyone on the staff has replaced the wandering flue. (Just in case you think that this particular candleholder is defective, they have switched it with other candleholders. On a different table, the flue remains in place, but whatever holder is on Table #2 invariably has the same problem!)

Recommendation

Don't hesitate to indulge in an excellent meal within the walls that once held Major André prisoner. In fact, it may be his famous restless spirit causing some of the haunted activity, as he still waits for George Washington to grant a pardon and spare him the noose. (Or, it may be the aroma of the delicious pumpkin soup on a cold winter's day that attracts him—because it tastes so good it's enough to bring anyone out of their grave!)

There are few structures that survive today with the rich history of the Old '76 House, and fewer still that are open to the public. Enjoy the food, appreciate the history, and if you are seated at Table #2 and strange things happen, don't say you weren't warned!

Also take the time to look at the beautiful Manse house set back from the road just to the north of the Old '76 House, and the church and old cemetery across the street (where other spirits have been seen wandering).

To see the actual site of Major André's execution, turn left out of the front of the restaurant's parking lot and make your next left at the light. Then turn left on Andre Hill. A monument marks the spot of the hanging. The bizarre story behind this location follows.

Hours

Open every day.

Sunday: brunch 11 to 3 pm, dinner 4 to 9 pm. Monday-Thursday: lunch 11:30 am to 3 pm, dinner 5 to 9 pm. Friday: lunch 11:30 to 3, dinner 5 to 9:30 pm. Saturday: lunch 11:30 am to 3pm, dinner 5 to 10 pm.

Directions

From the 287/New York State Thruway: Take exit 12 to Route 303 south. After passing over the Palisades Parkway, turn right onto King's Highway at the next light. The road winds its way to a stop sign. Make a left and the restaurant will be just past the next light on your right.

From the Palisades Parkway: Take exit 5S to go south on Route 303, then follow the directions above to Kings Highway.

Major André's Place of Execution

Some people have claimed to see a spirit by this monument, and after understanding the events following his death, it would be no wonder if André wasn't resting in peace.

For forty years, only a humble pile of stones and a few trees were all there was to mark the grave of the man considered to be a hero in England. By 1821, the Duke of York felt that it was time to finally remove Major André from this foreign soil, and give him a proper resting place of honor in Westminster Abbey. It was hoped that all was forgotten, or at least forgiven, from the unpleasant business of the Revolutionary War—not to mention the more recent War of 1812.

The execution and original burial site of the British spy, Major John André.

Section 5

Unfortunately for the British consul, James Buchanan, who was sent to disinter the remains, the memories of treason and war had not been forgotten in Tappan. Some angry locals complained that paying such an honor to a British spy was a slap in the face to the hallowed memory of George Washington, and the situation threatened to get ugly. Buchanan, being a good Irishman, decided to use a bit of the blarney to smooth his way, and claimed that it was a custom in his country to have a few drinks before going to a cemetery. Not wishing to be completely disagreeable, the outspoken protestors took part in the custom—again and again, no doubt until most of them forgot what they had been protesting.

With the troublesome segment of the populace suitably inebriated and pacified, Buchanan quickly set to work exhuming the remains. Even here he was to run into a snag, as it was discovered that the roots of a peach tree planted by a sympathetic local woman had completely engulfed André's skull. There was no time to waste, however, and before the locals sobered up, the bones of the British spy had been carted away—at least, the majority of them. Some townspeople claimed that Buchanan's men worked in such haste that many of the smaller bones were left scattered across the ground. However, they were not there for long as eager souvenir hunters scooped them up.

While most of Major André was sent back to England, the site of his death and temporary burial remained marked only by a boulder. The farmer who placed the large stone there eventually regretted it, and grew tired of curiosity seekers trampling his fields and helping themselves to his fruit trees. He removed the stone and plowed over the site, hoping it would fade from memory.

In 1846, a simple carved stone with André's name and date of execution was placed near the spot, but by 1878, even that was gone. However, thanks to the recollections of several old-timers, the exact location was pinpointed. Cyrus Fields, the man who had made a fortune with the transatlantic cable, became interested in André and his story, and agreed to personally pay for the cost of a proper monument to be erected on the spot. On October 2, 1879, just a year shy of the 100th anniversary of the execution, the granite monument was dedicated.

Fields had actually envisioned a thirteen-acre, landscaped park around the monument, but the state and local historical societies declined both the offer of the land, and the idea. It seems that a century of time had not completely eradicated the resentment of the British and their spy. That resentment continued to build until it all came to an explosive head in February of 1882.

On Washington's birthday, a patriotic poet with the pen name of George Hendrix took a chisel to the monument. While the damage was minimal, Hendrix was undaunted. He returned a few weeks later with nitroglycerine, and the blast compromised André's monument to the extent that several people were able to knock it over. The monument was restored, but that was not the end of attempts to blow it up.

On Election Day in 1885, a loud explosion rocked the town. Dynamite had been used, and this time the base of the monument was demolished. For years the monument lay on its side, all but forgotten. When Cyrus Fields died in 1892, the property and monument were sold for back taxes—for the sum of only $6.55, to a former supervisor of the Town of Orangetown, George Dickey. Apparently, Dickey was not motivated by a sense of history, and sold the property to the American Scenic and Historic Preservation Society for $250—a tidy profit in the 1890s. The Preservation Society held the property until 1984, when it was given to Rockland County and became the first historic site in the County Park system.

After over 200 years, two explosions, and countless twists and turns, the site of one of America's most dramatic and historic events has hopefully written its last chapter. There may not be acres of landscaped gardens and long, tree-lined avenues leading to the monument, but it nonetheless stands as a remarkable symbol of our struggle for freedom, as well as all of the ensuing indiscretions that freedom enables.

The Bottom Line

The History: How can you resist the opportunity to visit one of America's most historic sites and have a great meal at the same time, and then take an after-dinner stroll to the site of the hanging of a notorious British spy? You really do feel like you are stepping back into colonial times with the architecture and décor, and you can easily picture George Washington being right at home wining and dining here.

The Haunting: People have seen a British officer, heard many inexplicable sounds, and witnessed objects moving. Ask for Table #2 if you want the best haunted seat in the house.

Maria's Rock.

Maria's Rock

In the days when Rockland consisted of tiny villages, sprawling farms and vast stretches of wilderness, a little girl named Maria picked up a basket and went to gather wild berries. It was a warm, inviting summer's day, and the reds and purples of the plump, ripe berries dotted the forest as far as she could see. So absorbed was Maria in finding the biggest and sweetest fruit, she didn't realize that she had wandered far from her home.

Maria called for her mother, but the only response was the sounds of the forest. She walked faster, then began to run, but in the tangle of underbrush and heavily wooded terrain, there was no way to tell which direction was home, and which direction took her deeper into danger. Exhausted, Maria climbed atop a large rock and cried herself to sleep.

By nightfall, Maria's mother frantically searched everywhere, calling her daughter's name over and over again. The only response was the lonely sounds of the forest.

It wasn't until autumn that they found Maria. She still lay atop the large rock, tatters of her dress still clinging to her bleached bones. For many years after, people passing by the rock could hear the sound of a young girl crying. Local children put flowers on Maria's Rock, trying to ease the suffering of the lost girl's spirit, but still the weeping continued.

As time passed, the wilderness disappeared. The land upon which rests Maria's Rock became the site for the sprawling Lederle Laboratories complex in Pearl River (which has been sold to another pharmaceutical company). But some people still claim that while driving down Middletown Road on a summer's evening, if you listen carefully as you pass the rock you can hear the sound of a young girl crying.

Recommendation

Please don't trespass onto company property to get to the rock. There's a good view of it from the road. (You can't miss it, as it is the only giant boulder on the lawn.)

Directions

From the New York State Thruway/I-287: At exit 13S, take ramp (right) onto the Palisades Interstate Parkway towards Palisades Parkway South/New Jersey. At exit 8W, take ramp (right) onto Route 59. Turn LEFT (south) onto Smith Street and turn LEFT onto ramp to Route 304. Take the first exit by turning RIGHT onto the ramp heading north on Middletown Road, Pearl River. The large campus of the pharmaceutical company will be on your left. Maria's Rock is roughly in the center of the front lawn.

The Bottom Line

The History: A young girl was found dead on the rock. It's a popular local story that has been around for many generations, but like many such stories there is no documented evidence.

The Haunting: Most of the reports of hearing a girl crying at the rock were before the area and the company became so developed. Still worth taking some photos and seeing if anything turns up.

Section 5

MOUNT MOOR
CEMETERY

This "Burying ground for Colored people" was deeded on July 7, 1849 by James Benson, and Jane Benson, his wife, to William H. Moore, Stephen Samuels and Isaac Williams, trustees. The cemetery has provided burial space for colored people, including veterans of the Civil War, the Spanish - American War, World Wars I and II and the Korean War. The grounds have been maintained since 1940 by the Mount Moor Cemetery Association, Inc.

Stores close to the cemetery have reported a shadowy figure.

Mount Moor Cemetery

The Palisades Center was built around
Mount Moor Cemetery.

The Palisades Center mall in West Nyack is unique in several regards—it is one of the largest malls in the country, since it opened ten years ago, there have been persistent rumors that the entire structure is sinking, and there are many people buried on the property. No doubt it is the latter fact that makes the Palisades Center a most unusual shopping destination. After all, how many other malls have cemeteries in the middle of their parking lots?

Mount Moor Cemetery predates the mall by almost 150 years, and due to its historic nature, there was no way the bodies would have been relocated, so the mall and parking lots were built around the cemetery. The significance of the site is that it is a rare African-American cemetery containing the remains of several generations of veterans.

The historic marker at Mount Moor reads:

"Burying ground for Colored people, was deeded on July 7, 1849 by James Benson and Jane Benson his wife to William H. Moor, Stephen Samuels and Isaac Williams, trustees. The cemetery has provided burial space for colored people, including veterans of the Civil War, the Spanish American War, World Wars I and II and the Korean War. The grounds have been maintained since 1940 by the Mount Moor Cemetery Association, Inc."

Among these veterans is a member of the 54th Massachusetts (the African-American regiment in the Civil War made famous by the movie *Glory*), and six of the renowned Buffalo Soldiers. Unfortunately, the site is rarely noticed by the average busy shopper, and those who do catch site of the grave stones have no clue of the cemetery's historic importance.

That being said, shoppers and mall employees have noticed things that may be connected to the cemetery, in a hauntingly strange kind of way. Since the mall opened, there have been many reports of shadowy figures in one of the large stores closest to the cemetery. When the store is first opened early in the morning, or late at night after closing, a figure has been seen moving through the store, but upon investigation, no one is ever found.

Recommendation

The cemetery has a small parking area near the gate. You can also explore the adjacent parking garage and some of the nearby stores and see if your sixth sense tells you anything. And during or after a long day of haunted sites touring, this is the ideal place to get just about any kind of food you can imagine in mall's large food court or in one of the many restaurants.

Directions

The Palisades Center is at Exit 12 of the New York State Thruway. Mount Moor Cemetery is located on the south side of the mall in front of the parking garage and Barnes & Noble.

The Bottom Line

The History: Mount Moor is a historic African-American cemetery where several generations of veterans are buried.

The Haunting: Shadowy figures are seen in a nearby store.

Section 5

Every high school has its terrifying legends, tall tales that are usually short on facts. For instance, an infamous path through the woods where students disappear, or an annual dance from which one unlucky participant will never return alive. In the 1950s, one Rockland County high school circulated a classic cemetery legend involving the Old Brick Church in Spring Valley.

This beautiful church in a picturesque setting was built in 1774, and its cemetery contains the graves of both Revolutionary War and Civil War soldiers. Like most places in the Hudson Valley, housing developments have encroached on the edges of the property, disturbing what once must have been such a tranquil spot for contemplation. Or was it something quite different, especially at sunset?

The Brick Church.

Section 5

There is a story that a fifteen-year-old girl was murdered behind the church in the 1920s or 30s. From that day, mothers warned their daughters to stay clear of the churchyard at night. A legend soon arose that if a fifteen-year-old girl was present at sunset, you would be able to hear the phantom scream of the murdered girl.

As crazy as this seems, dozens of eyewitnesses over the course of generations have heard the sunset scream. An old Packard automobile from the 20s or 30s has also been seen driving slowly through the cemetery, and then disappearing. In recent years, many people claim to have recorded strange things, such as whispering or talking sounds coming from the ground.

Recommendation

Drive by any time of the day to enjoy this beautiful church and explore the old cemetery, but plan to be there around sunset if you want to try to hear or record the scream. Look for the graves Revolutionary War and Civil War veterans, as well as the family plots of some of the area's earliest families.

PLEASE NOTE: This is still an active church, so please do not disrupt any services that may be in progress. Also, as this is church property, please do not trespass on the premises at night.

Visitor Information

Brick Church
220 Brick Church Road
Spring Valley, New York 10977

This is an active church, not a museum. There are no regularly scheduled tours or events.

Directions

From the New York State Thruway (I-287):
At exit 14B, turn onto ramp towards Airmont Road/Airmont/Montebello. Turn south on North Airmont Road toward Route 59. (If you were heading south on the Thruway, you would turn right at the end of the ramp. Heading north, make a left off the exit.) Turn LEFT (East) onto Route 59. Proceed 2.4 miles and turn LEFT onto Main Street (name changes to Route 306). In about 2.3 miles, turn RIGHT onto Brick Church Road. The church will be on your LEFT.

The Bottom Line

The History: The church was built in 1774. The cemetery contains the graves of Revolutionary War and Civil War soldiers, as well as many of the earliest families from the area.

The Haunting: A murdered girl's scream is heard at sunset, there's an old car that disappears, and voices come from the ground.

One of the Hudson Valley's oldest ghost stories involves the spirit of a girl murdered at Spook Rock.

Spook Rock

One of the oldest ghost stories in Rockland County is set on Spook Rock Road in Airmont. Over the generations this story has acquired so many variations that only two elements remain consistent—a rock and a ghost.

Spook is an old Dutch term meaning spirit and the story does involve some of the earliest Dutch settlers in the county. As the story goes, one of the settlers committed some kind of crime against the local Indian population. Whatever the alleged deed, the result was that the Indians decided to seek revenge. They kidnapped the young daughter of the settler and brought her to the rock, which they used for ceremonies. At the time, there was a cave beneath the rock and the top of the rock had a large indentation that would have been ideal for a fire.

After conducting the appropriate revenge ceremony (which may or may not have involved dancing and chanting depending upon the version one hears), the innocent girl was sacrificed on the rock. Almost immediately after the terrible deed was done, members of the tribe learned that the father was not guilty of the crime for which he had been accused. This left the chief with terrible feelings of guilt and remorse, and some versions of the story say that the ghost of the murdered girl haunted him every night of his life, visible only to him.

There is also a version that claims that the girl's spirit was seen by all the members of the tribe, hovering over the rock where her unjust death occurred, either strictly on the anniversary of the sacrifice, or every night until every member of the tribe had died. Her ghost was described as being everything from a simple glowing form drifting above the rock, to a vengeful, angry spirit that drew people like an irresistible magnet, never allowing a peaceful night for the rest of their lives.

In more modern times, some people claimed to have seen a ghostly figure hovering above the rock. These sightings have most often occurred around Halloween, the time around which the legend claims the sacrifice took place. Many local residents have also insisted that the road leading to the rock has an eerie feeling to it. This in part was the result of the illusion that cars put in neutral could roll uphill, as if being mysteriously and magnetically pulled toward the rock.

Recommendation

Like so many other places, the modern world has encroached on Spook Rock, which is now reinforced with bricks and concrete. With the volume of traffic in the area, for safety sake, please don't try putting your car in neutral to see if you can roll uphill. It is also not safe to stop your car by the rock, so find a side street and carefully walk back along the road if you want to take pictures. Indian Rock is a short distance from here, so make sure you check out both locations.

Directions

From the New York State Thruway: Take exit 14B and go north on North Airmont Road. After passing Pioneer Avenue on you right, Spook Rock will be at the corner of the next intersection on Spook Rock Road. If you are sitting in the intersection, the rock is to your right across the street.

From Route 59: Turn north on North Airmont Road and follow the directions above.

The Bottom Line

The History: It is believed that Spook Rock was a Native American ceremonial site, and it was on an Indian trail that led from upstate New York to Mahwah, New Jersey. There is no documented evidence of a Dutch girl being killed at this site, but it is one of the oldest stories in the area.

The Haunting: The spirit of a girl is seen over the rock. Cars allegedly roll uphill toward the rock.

Do angry Native American spirits still inhabit the land around Indian Rock?

Indian Rock

FIRE

Long ago, there was an old Indian trail that began in upstate New York and went through Rockland County, passing by Spook Rock, Indian Rock, and on to the tribal meeting place in Mahwah, New Jersey. Indian Rock was also a local landmark for generations of more recent Rocklanders who grew up in the area.

Indian Rock was almost pulverized when a local developer tried to renege on a previous agreement to leave it intact, but a local groundswell of support saved it. The shopping center eventually went up around the rock, which is now enclosed in a fence to prevent people from climbing on top or from crawling into the opening inside of the rock.

The first business to be built on the Indian Rock land was a McDonalds. Rumors quickly spread of haunted activity and customers continue to report strange electrical anomalies and odd sensations. Perhaps some of the other stores also have haunted activity, but often businesses are reluctant to speak about such things.

Behind the row of stores adjacent to the rock are condos where some residents are fearful of going to the lower level as they sense a strong presence watching them. These residents had no prior knowledge of the spooky reputation of Indian Rock and the surrounding area, so it wasn't cases of overactive imaginations.

As this was the location of a site connected to Native Americans, and activity didn't seem to occur until development began and the rock was threatened, some people speculate that it is angered Indian spirits that make their presence known here. Of course it is all speculation, but there have been enough independent reports that it appears to be more than a mere coincidence.

Recommendation

Being so close to Spook Rock, its convenient to visit both locations, especially if you have an interest in Native American landmarks. People have had odd experiences both inside the McDonalds and at the drive-thru window. While you can't directly access the rock because of the fence, it's worth taking a close look, and imagining hundreds of years ago when Indians walked past this once heavily-wooded spot, and perhaps huddled deep within the rock for shelter.

Directions

Indian Rock is located in a shopping center of the same name on the westbound side of Route 59 in Suffern, just to the east of Good Samaritan Hospital. For GPS navigation, the address of the McDonalds is 1 Indian Rock, Suffern, New York.

From the New York State Thruway: At exit 14B, turn South onto Airmont Road toward Route 59. Turn RIGHT onto Route 59. Indian Rock is 0.8 miles on your RIGHT.

The Bottom Line

The History: While there is no proof that Indian Rock had any religious or ceremonial significance to Native Americans, it was no doubt a landmark for traveling tribes.

The Haunting: The feeling of a strong presence in nearby homes and businesses. Electrical devices are known to act erratically, especially in and around the McDonalds.

Section 5

Places Index